LIBRARY MANAGEMENT AND ADMINISTRATION

ESSENTIALS OF LIBRARY MANAGEMENT AND ADMINISTRATION

ANIL KAPOOR

PhD (Library & Information Science), M. Phil (Library Science), M.Lib Science, B.Lib Science, Master in Arts (M.V) & Master of Philosophy (M.V)

Ess Ess Publications

New Delhi

ESSENTIALS OF LIBRARY MANAGEMENT AND ADMINISTRATION

ISBN: 978-81-934311-1-5

First Published 2017

Published by:
Ess Ess Publications
4831/24, Ansari Road,
Darya Ganj,
New Delhi-110 002.
INDIA
Phones: 23260807, 41563444
Fax: 41563334
E-mail: info@essessreference.com
www.essessreference.com

Cover Design by *Patch Creative Unit*

Printed and bound in India

To the glory of God
"the almighty",
without whom I am nothing
&
To my family
for their endless support
and encouragement.

Contents

Acknowledgements

Success is the fruit of hard work. This book was possible due to the collective efforts of so many personalities to whom I wish to express my gratitude.

First and foremost, I would like to humbly thank almighty God for his divine intervention in my life without which I would not have been able to make this study.

Transcending all this, I wish to acknowledge the sweet love, affection and care of my grandparents Sh. Mela Ram, Smt. Maya Devi and Sh. Tek Chand, Smt. Maya Devi who have been like a spring of inspiration and strength for me.

I owe deep gratitude to my father Sh. SomNath and mother Smt. Shanti Devi. Their constant inspiration and guidance kept me focused and motivated. They bore me, raised me, supported me, taught me and loved me. the support of my elder brother, Dr. Ajay Kapoor is sincerely acknowledged. Words fail to express my appreciation to my wife Pooja Kapoor and son Aryan Kapoor whose dedication and persistent confidence in me has taken the load off my shoulders.

I am thankful to my elder sisters, Mrs. Meenakshi, Sangeeta and Anju who assisted me directly or indirectly in completion of this book.

— Anil Kapoor

Preface

Leadership and management are two vital components in any profession. There are high expectations of these components from professional library personnel because of the increasing demands of library and the institutions. Library personnel have multifunctional roles in teaching institutions and in library, so they must possess good knowledge and skills in leadership and management to work efficiently as good managers for smooth running of the organization. This book results from continued strong belief in the need for a text that focuses on library leadership and management issues of present and future in a distinctive pattern. This edition is incorporated with many suggestions from both library service and library education fronts, as it focuses on the critical roles of leaders and managers. This book has been written for diploma of library science, bachelor of library science and can be used as a reference tool for post-graduate students of library and information science. This book covers all the topics of management in the library science curriculum and is in accordance with the syllabi of major Indian universities. This text is grounded with theoretical and practical aspects of leadership and management in library science education, library practice and library administration.

This book can facilitate new learners to get acquainted with the basic knowledge of leadership and management which can be applied in practical aspects of academics and library area. I have tried to explain the concepts in a simple and comprehensive manner to develop a foundation for new library professionals. This book will help in managing such leadership aspects in their practical life in library profession as it will help them to understand the basic concepts of management and leadership in simple terms.

The chapters have been sequentially placed to facilitate ease of reading and understanding. This textbook is divided into six units, with each unit focusing on one of the major domains of library management.

UNIT 1: INTRODUCTION TO LIBRARY MANAGEMENT

Management : Introduction, Definitions of Management, Characteristics of Management, Nature of Management, Various Concept of Good Management, Management Theories, Level of Management, Elements of Management, Principles of Management, Henri Fayol's 14 Principles and their Implication in Today's Library & Information Centres (LICs).

Scientific Management : Introduction, Definitions of Scientific Management, Principles of Scientific Management, An Outline Structure of Taylor's Scientific Management, Application of Scientific Management Principles to Libraries, Value of Scientific Management to Libraries.

Administration : Introduction, Meaning of Administration, Definitions of Administration, Philosophy of Administration, Scope of Administration, Importance of Administration, Nature of Administration, Difference between Management and Administration, Significance of Library Administration.

UNIT 2: MANAGEMENT PROCESS

Planning : Introduction, Definition of Planning, Components of Planning, Purpose of Planning, Classification of Planning, Characteristics of Planning,

Basic Principles of Planning, Types of Planning, Advantages of Planning, Limitations of Planning, Step of Planning in Library, Planning in Library Management.

Staffing : Introduction, Definition of Staffing, Nature of Staffing Function of Staffing, Steps Involved in Staffing, Need of Staffing, Importance of Staffing, Factors of Staffing, Role of Library Manager in Staffing.

HRM : Introduction, Concept of HRM, Definitions of HRM, Nature of HRM, Scope of HRM, Objectives of HRM, Functions of HRM, HRM-Key Responsibilities, Process of HRM.

Recruitment : Introduction, Definition of Recruitment, Importance of Recruitment, Purpose of Recruitment, Needs of Recruitment, Process of Recruitment, Sources of Recruitment, Advantages of Recruitment through Internal Sources, Methods of Recruitment, Policy of Recruitment.

Selection : Introduction, Meaning of Selection, Definition of Selection, Significance of Selection, Steps of Selection, Approval by the appropriate authority and issuing of appointment letter, Difference between recruitment and selection.

Job Analysis : Introduction, Concepts, Job, Meaning of Job Analysis, Definition of Job Analysis, Types of Job Analysis, Methods of Job Analysis, Purpose of Job Analysis, Process of Job Analysis.

Job Description : Introduction, Definition of Job description, Roles and Responsibilities of Job description, Purposes of Job description in library, General and Specific Purpose of Job description, Limitations of Job description, Job Content/Writing Job description, Steps of Job description, Principles of Job description.

Job Evaluation : Introduction, Meaning of Job Evaluation, Definition of Job Evaluation, Process of Job Evaluation, Objectives of Job Evaluation, Method of Job Evaluation, Principles of Job Evaluation, Limitations of

Job Evaluation.

Performance Appraisal : Introduction, Meaning of Performance Appraisal, Definition of Performance Appraisal, Characteristics of Performance Appraisal, Objectives of Performance Appraisal, Advantages of Performance Appraisal.

Training and Development : Introduction, Meaning of Training, Meaning of Development, Concept of Training and Development, Definition of Training, Definition of Training and Development, Importance of Training and Development, Reasons to go for Training and Development, Need of Training and Development, HR Role of Training and Development, Objectives of Training and Development, Difference between Training and Development, Traditional and Modern Approach of Training and Development, Methods of Training and Development.

UNIT 3: LIBRARY ENVIRONMENT

Library Committee: Introduction, Meaning of Library Committee, Definition of Library Committee, Types of Library Committee, Need of Library Committee, Functions and Power of Library Committee, Characteristics of Library Committee, Responsibilities of the Librarian toward Library Committee.

Library Organizational Structure : Introduction of Library Organizational, Library Organizational Structure.

Ranganathan Staff Formula : Introduction, Development of Staffing Patterns, Status of Staffing Pattern, Ranganathan Staff Formula, Staff Pattern for Public Libraries

UNIT 4: MOTIVATIONAL PATTERNS

Motivation : Introduction, Meaning of Motivation, Traditional and Modern Approach of Motivation, Definition of Motivation, Characteristics of Motivation, Need and Importance of Motivation, Process of Motivation, Sources of Motivation, Theories of Motivation, Maslow's Theory, ERG THEORY, Herzberg's Two-Factor Theory, McClelland's Theory of Needs, Douglas McGregor Theory of "X" AND "Y", Goal Setting Theory, Reinforcement Theory, Equity Theory.

UNIT 5: LIBRARY PLANNING

Library Planning : Introduction of library planning, Tools and Techniques of Library Planning, Benefits of a Plan, Recipe for a Plan, Phases of a Proposed Library Building, Planning Responsibilities, Some Conceptual Principles of Planning with Modern Libraries.

Total Quality Management : Introduction, TQM, Definition, Models of Total Quality Management, Quality Management Tools, Fourteen Steps to TQM, Concept of Library Quality, Benefits of Quality Management in Libraries, Quality Indicators in Libraries, Quality Management in Libraries, Role of Library Managers in TQM, Principles of TQM in Libraries, Elements of TQM, Applications of TQM in Libraries, Benefits of TQM in Libraries, Best Practices for Implementation of TQM in Libraries, Barriers to Implementing to TQM in Libraries

Quality Standard : Introduction, What is Quality, ISO-9000 Origin, Aspects of Quality Systems, Structure of ISO-9000, Quality Procedure, Elements of ISO-9000, Benefits from ISO-9000 Certification, The University Library Quality Assurance System, Conclusion.

UNIT 6: SYSTEM ANALYSIS AND CONTROL

System Analysis : Introduction of System Analysis, Meaning of System, Definitions of System, Systems Analysis, Analysis, Characteristics of a System, Elements of a System, Types of System, Steps of System Analysis.

Systems Design : Introduction of System Design, General Considerations of System Design, Steps of Design, Conclusion.

Budgeting : Introduction, Historical Background

of Budget, Meaning of Budget, Definition of Budget, Definition of Budgeting, Essentials of a Budget, Characteristics of Budget, Types of Budgets, Purpose, Functions, Advantages, Principles, Budgeting Techniques of Financial Planning, Budgeting Planning for Library, Budgeting planning factors for Library, Steps for Budgeting Process, Librarian's role under fund crisis, Conclusion.

Evaluation Techniques : Introduction, Goals of Evaluation, Types of Evaluation, Evaluation Procedures, Methods of Evaluation, Evaluation Techniques.

Hope this book will be beneficial for the library science students to maximum extent possible as a result of the dedication and hard work put up to make it more understandable for the beginner leaders and managers.

— Anil Kapoor

Unit I
LIBRARY MANAGEMENT

- ***Management:*** *Introduction, Definitions of Management, Characteristics of Management, Nature of Management, Various Concept of Good Management, Management Theories, Level of Management, Elements of Management, Principles of Management, Henri Fayol's 14 Principles and their Implication in Today's Library & Information Centres (LICs).*
- ***Scientific Management:*** *Introduction, Definitions of Scientific Management, Principles of Scientific Management, An Outline Structure of Taylor's Scientific Management, Application of Scientific Management Principles to Libraries, Value of Scientific Management to Libraries.*
- ***Administration:*** *Introduction, Meaning of Administration, Definitions of Administration, Philosophy of Administration, Scope of Administration, Importance of Administration, Nature of Administration, Difference between Management and Administration, Significance of Library Administration.*

INTRODUCTION TO MANAGEMENT IN LIBRARY SCIENCE

MANAGEMENT

INTRODUCTION

Management is the scientific art of achieving the results of goals by effective utilization of the resources. Management is a science which has made tremendous contributions to the improvement of all the industry including library science. As the library is a core industry in today's world and we are having united resources, so it has become a great need to use these resources efficiently with meticulous managerial skills. Management generally lays emphasis on control i.e. control of personnel, control of cost, time, salaries, overtime, inventory etc. Management is required to plan, organize, co-ordinate and control the affairs of the organization. It brings the human and material resources together and motivates people for achievement of the objectives of the organization. Management is a universal process in all social and economic activities. Management is involved to some extent in all activities of human life.

DEFINITIONS

Management in general can be defined as all the activities and tasks undertaken by one or more persons for the purpose of planning and controlling the activities of others in order to achieve an objective or complete an activity that could not be acting independently.

According to F.W. Taylor, "Management is the art of knowing what you want to do and then seeing that they do it in the best and the cheapest may."

According to Peter Drucker, "Management is a multipurpose organ that manages a business and manages Managers and manages Workers and work."

According to George R. Terry, "Management Is a distinct process consisting of planning, organizing, actuating and controlling, utilizing in each both science and art, and followed in order to accomplish pre-determined objectives."

According to Harold Koontz, "Management is the art of getting things done through others and with formally organized groups."

According to Mary Parker Follett, "Management is the art of getting things done through people."

CHARACTERISTICS OF MANAGEMENT

- Management is a profession as it has a systematic and specialized body of knowledge consisting of principles and techniques which can be taught as a separate discipline.
- Management is a group activity as it makes people realize the objectives of the group and directs their efforts towards the achievement of these goals.
- Management is universal in nature as it is applicable in all types of organizations.
- Management is goal oriented as it exists to achieve some definite goals and objectives.

- Management is a dynamic function as it has to be performed continuously to mould the organization as per the changing business environment.

NATURE OF MANAGEMENT

- Management is a scientific process by which objectives of an organization are observed in a planned way.
- Management is a process to allocate and utilize the resources efficiently.
- Management is the managerial process of forming a strategic vision, setting objectives, crafting a strategy and then implementing and executing the strategy.
- Management means deciding what is to be done and getting the work done by other people who are brought into a group to work harmoniously and efficiently to accomplish common laid down organizational objectives.
- Management focuses on the entire organizational process from both a short and a long term perspective.
- Management is a functional concept and persons performing management are designated as managers or executives.

VARIOUS CONCEPT OF GOOD MANAGEMENT

- It is a profession.
- It is a dynamic function.
- It is a social process.
- It is a universal in character.
- It is always goal oriented.
- It is a group activity.
- It is multidisciplinary.

MANAGEMENT THEORIES

The current management practices have evolved from earlier theories. Management practices were actually a part of the governance in ancient times. Most of the current understanding of management however is based on the classical theories of management that were introduced in 1800s during industrial age.

1. Classical Management Theory : It is the oldest theory and is sometimes referred to as traditional management theory. The classical perspective includes three subfields of management: scientific management, bureaucratic management and administrative management (Wren, 1979).

- **Scientific Management Theory:** In this theory, the focus is on the goals and productivity. The organization is viewed as a machine to be run efficiently to increase production. Managers must closely supervise the work to assure maximum efficiency. Workers must have proper tools and equipments. There is a focus on training the workers to work more efficiently and performance incentives are used. Time and motion studies are the vehicle for determining how to do and organize the work in the most efficient manner.

- **Bureaucratic Management Theory :** The focus of this theory is on the superior subordinate communication transmitted from top to bottom via a clear chain of command, a hierarchy of authority and division of labor chain. This theory uses rational and impersonal management process. Here, there are explicit rules and regulations for the governing activities, focusing on exacting work processes and technical competence. There is a use of merit and skill as the basis for promotion or reward. The emphasis is given on lifetime career service and salaried managers.

- **Administrative Management Theory :** Here, the focus is on the science of management and principles of an organization applicable in any setting. It identifies the needs for 'POSDCORB' where P stand for Planning, O for Organizing, S for Staffing, D for Directing, Co for Co-ordination, R for Reporting and B for Budgeting. It is mainly concerned with the optimal approach for administrators to achieve economic efficiency.

2. Human Relation Management Theory : In this theory, the focus is on the empowerment of the individual worker as a source of control, motivation and productivity in the organizations. The Hawthorne studies led to belief that human relation between workers and managers and among the workers were the main determinants of efficiency. The Hawthorne effect refers to the phenomena of how being observed or studied results in a change of behavior. This theory also emphasizes on the participatory decision making which increases worker's autonomy. It also lays emphasis on the training of the employees to improve work.

LEVEL OF MANAGEMENT

The level of management means arranged managerial positions in an organization. The main significance of levels of management determines authority relationships in an organization. On the basis of authority and responsibility three levels are identified i.e. Top Management, Middle Management and Lower Management. The management of a large organization may have about three levels:

1. Top Management
2. Middle Management
3. Lower Management

1. Top Management : General policies are laid down by the top ranking officials in a management system the (Chief) Librarian. These are called chief or top executives, who issue necessary orders, instructions and give advice from time to time to their subordinates so as to see that the directions or policies are properly executed for attaining the objectives of the enterprise. They are directly responsible to the library committee about the progress made or the failure of the plans executed by them.

Functions of Top Management

- Determine the objectives and goals of organization.
- Formulating policies and strategies and making plans to achieve the objectives lay.
- Setting up an organizational framework.
- Defining procedures for manpower and material management.
- Stating rules and regulations for effective control.

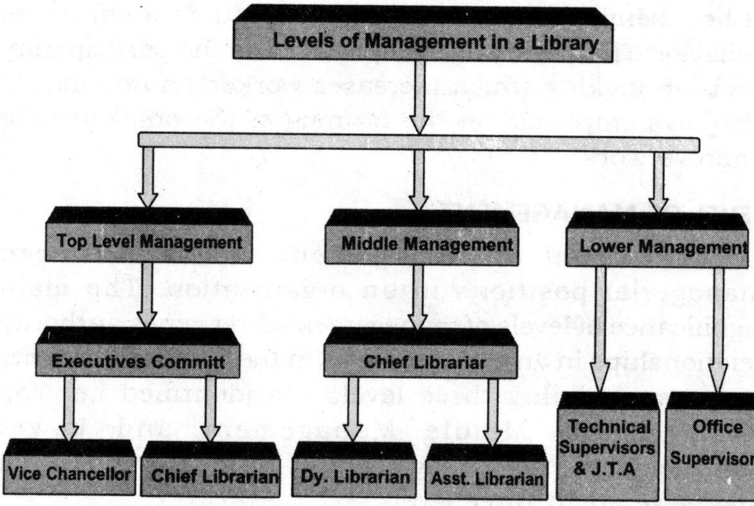

2. Middle Management : There are employee executing and interpreting the policies though out the library. Such persons are not the policy-makers but the followers of the policies. They take responsibility of the successful operations of divisions and departments. They are heads of the department divisions. The middle management is an important link in the management structure. They are the persons communicating the orders of the top level to the lower level. Their right interpretation and its implementation can take the library to the high peak of the utility.

Functions of Middle Level Management

- Interpret and state the policies framed by the top level management.
- Preparation of organizational set up in their respective departments.
- Assigning duties and responsibilities to the staff for timely execution of the formulated plans.
- Selecting best persons for different tasks according to their knowledge, experience and expertise.
- Giving instructions to the departmental heads regarding the work force.
- Motivating personnel to achieve higher productivity.
- Collecting reports of work from various departments the task performed and further reporting to top level management.
- Putting up recommendations to the top level management for better implementation of plans and policies.
- Supervision and timely performance appraisal of the work done.

3. Lower Level Management : It includes the supervisory persons. Lower management is also called with the name of 'supervisory management'. The lower management has also got a strong and valuable position in the library because final execution of the policies is carried out by the employees work under their supervision or direction. Lower management is directly responsible to the middle management, office-supervisor and section-supervisors. The lower executive therefore, acts as the representative of the working staff. In other words, Lower management is a link between the middle management and the working staff.

Functions of operating management are enlisted below:

- To maintain discipline in the unit.
- To communicate the grievances of the staff to higher level of management if remain unresolved.
- To direct the workers about the procedure protocols and solving their problems whenever required.
- To control and supervise the performance of the workers.
- To arrange adequate quantity of materials and equipments and ensuring the quality of equipments for the work force.
- To assign the suitable personnel for various works to execute the work efficiently.
- To plan day to day work within the goals prescribed by higher level management.

ELEMENTS OF MANAGEMENT

Management has been described as a social process involving responsibility for economical and effective planning and regulation of operation of an enterprise in the fulfillment of given purposes. It is a dynamic process consisting of various elements and activities. These activities are different from operative functions like marketing, finance, purchase etc. Rather these activities are common to each and every manager irrespective of his level or status.

Different experts have classified functions of management. According to George and Jerry, "There are four fundamental functions/elements of management i.e. planning, organizing, actuating and controlling". According to Henry Fayol, "To manage is to forecast and plan, to organize, to command, and to control". Whereas Luther Gullick has given a pneumonic "**POSDCORB**' where P stand for Planning, O for Organizing, S for Staffing, D for Directing, Co for Co-ordination, R for Reporting and B for Budgeting.

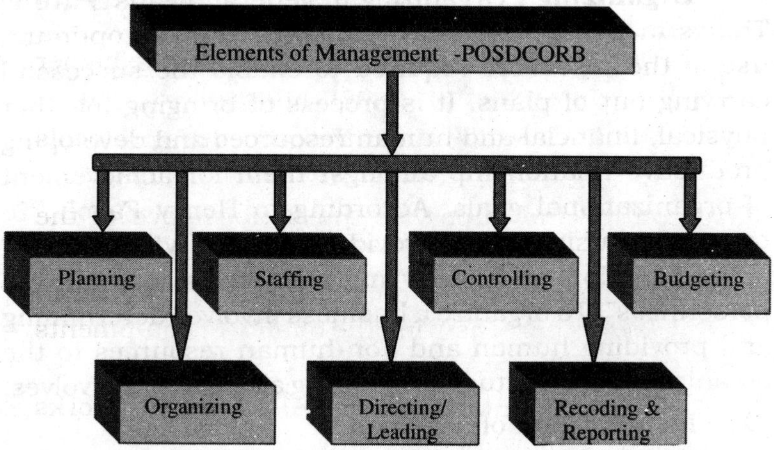

Planning : Planning is deciding what needs to happen in the future (today, next week, next month, next year, over the next years, etc.) and generating plans for action. It is the basic elements of management. It deals with chalking out a future course of action and deciding in advance the most appropriate course of actions for achievement of pre-determined goals. According to Koontz, "Planning is deciding in advance-what to do, when to do and how to do. It bridges the gap from where we are and where we want to be". A plan is a future course of actions. It is an exercise in problem solving and decision making. Planning is determination of courses of action to achieve desired goals. Thus, planning is a systematic thinking about ways and means for accomplishment of pre-determined goals. Planning is necessary to ensure proper utilization of human and non-human resources. It is all pervasive, an intellectual activity and helps in avoiding confusion, uncertainties, risks, wastages etc.

In library planning, the locality, its make up as regards its physical features, its linguistic divisions, its cultural diversities and educational needs etc. are taken into account before providing a service. The pros and cons are properly studied so that the service is effective and long enduring.

Organizing : Organizing in general means 'Putting Things in Order'. Organizing is done to make optimum use of the resources required to enable the successful carrying out of plans. It is process of bringing together physical, financial and human resources and developing productive relationship amongst them for achievement of organizational goals. According to Henry Fayol, "To organize a business is to provide it with everything useful or its functioning i.e. raw material, tools, capital and personnel's". To organize a business involves determining and providing human and non-human resources to the organizational structure. Organizing as a process involves:

1. Identification of activities.
2. Classification of grouping of activities.
3. Assignment of duties.
4. Delegation of authority and creation of responsibility.
5. Coordinating authority and responsibility relationships.

In library organization, the decision is taken as to what kind of authority is to be provided for an area of service. Should be authority the autonomous or part and parcel of the local government machinery. If it is to be autonomous of the local government authority, it is to be found out as to whether this autonomous body would be capable of raising and collecting enough finances for running the library.

Staffing : Staffing in an organization means job analyzing, recruitment and hiring individuals for appropriate jobs. It is the function of manning the organization structure and keeping it manned. Staffing has assumed greater importance in the recent years due to advancement of technology increase in size of business, complexity of human behavior etc. The main purpose of staffing is to put right man on right job i.e. square pegs in square holes and round pegs in round holes. According to Kootz and O'Donell, "Managerial functional of staffing involving manning the organization structure through proper and effective selection, appraisal and development of personnel to fill the roles designed in the structure".

Staffing involves:

1. Promotions and transfers.
2. Performance appraisal.
3. Remuneration.
4. Training and development.
5. Recruitment, selection and placement.
6. Manpower planning (estimating man power in terms of searching, choosing the person and giving the right place in the organization).

The chief librarian of a public library should be sympathetic towards readers and should be capable of understanding the varied tasted of the public. Besides advanced learning, he should be able to common respect by his qualities of leadership. He should be a competent person to serve as a public relations officer i.e. to serve as a liaison officer between the readers and the books. The common people consider him a guide and the librarian should come up to their expectations.

Directing/Leading : Directing means determining what needs to be done in a situation and getting people to do it. It is that part of managerial function which actuates the organizational methods to work efficiently for achievement of organizational purposes. It is considered life-spark of the enterprise which sets it in motion the action of people because planning, organizing and staffing are the mere preparations for doing the work. Direction is that inert-personnel aspect of managerial which deals directly with influencing, guiding, supervising, motivating sub-ordinate for the achievement of organizational goals. Direction has following elements:

1. Supervision : It implies overseeing the work of subordinates by their superiors. It is the act of watching and directing work and workers.

2. Motivation : It means inspiring, stimulating or encouraging the sub-ordinates with zeal to work. Positive, negative, monetary, non-monetary incentives may be used for this purpose.

3. Leadership : It may be defined as a process by which manager guides and influences the work of subordinates in desired direction.

4. Communication : It is the process of passing information, experience, opinion etc., from one person to another. It is a bridge of understanding between the personnel in any organization for its smooth functioning.

The harmony and efficiency of the staff depends upon the personal qualities of the chief librarian. He should be capable of performing his duties as a leader. It implies that besides possessing knowledge, he should be able to boost up their morale. He should be an example to be followed by his subordinates. In other words, he should not be frustrated with his job. Rather, he should do his job with zeal. He should be ready to sacrifice his personal comforts for the sake of library work and library staff. He should prove an ideal leader by dint of his hard work and sincerity for the staff welfare. Directing includes continuous decision making and embodying them in general and specific orders and instructions.

Controlling/Monitoring : Controlling means checking progress against plans. It implies measurement of accomplishment against the standards and correction of deviation if any to ensure achievement of organizational goals. The purpose of controlling is to ensure that everything occurs in conformity with the standards. An efficient system of control helps to predict deviations before they actually occur. According to Theo Haimann, "Controlling is the process of checking whether or not proper progress is being made towards the objectives, goals and acting if necessary, to correct any deviation". According to Koontz and O'Donell, "Controlling is the measurement and correction of performance activities of subordinates in order to make sure that the enterprise objectives and plans desired to obtain them as being accomplished". Therefore, controlling has following steps:

1. Corrective action.
2. Comparison of actual performance with the standards and finding out deviation if any.
3. Measurement of actual performance.
4. Establishment of standard performance.

Co-ordination : Co-ordination is the unification, integration, synchronization of the efforts of group members so as to provide unity of action in the pursuit of common goals. It is a hidden force which binds all the other functions of management. According to Mooney and Reelat, "Co-ordinate is orderly arrangement of group efforts to provide unity of action in the pursuit of common goals. According to Charles Worth, "Co-ordinate is the integration of several parts into an orderly whole to achieve the purpose of understanding". Co-ordinate is an orderly arrangement of efforts to provide unity of action in the fulfillment of common objective whereas co-operation denotes collective efforts of persons working in an enterprise voluntarily for the achievement of a particular purpose. It is the willingness of individuals to help each other. Coordination is an effort to integrate effectively energies of different group whereas co-operation is sort to achieve general objectives of business.

Recording and Reporting : Records are piece of evidence about the past incidents, e.g. Library record. Recording and reporting is keeping informed those to whom the executive is responsible, as to what is going on, which thus includes keeping himself and his subordinates informed through records, research and inspections. Recording is a document of facts and records are a means of communication between the care providers in respect of the care provided to the clients. Reporting is a process of keeping the superior informed to whom the subordinates are responsible and accountable. Reports consist of written and verbal communication between and amongst concerned personnel and reports are an account given about a particular can therefore be accessed through reporting system. Records and reports should be accurate, complete, and up-to-date, organized and must be kept confidential.

The chief of a library has to submit an annual report to the executive authority concerned. This practice keeps the chief vigilant about his own activities since he knows that somebody else above him is keeping a watch upon him. Laski, a renowned political philosopher, observed, Vigilance is the price of freedom. The chief librarian, in turn, has to ask various section heads of his library to maintain proper records and statistics of the work performed by their respective subordinates so that a faithful and factual report is presented to the former.

Budgeting : Budgeting is all that goes with fiscal planning, accounting and controlling of financial resources. Budgeting can be prepared based on the previous financial documents and planning new activities of the coming year. Its functions are to identify the importance of short and long term fiscal plans that reflects the unit needs. It articulates and documents unit needs effectively to higher administrative levels. It demonstrates knowledge of budgeting and uses appropriate techniques of fiscal planning accounting and controlling. It provides subordinates the opportunities to participate in fiscal planning and use of funds properly. Budgeting involves recording income expenditure and the surplus which is kept as record for future use.

The libraries have been given almost the lowest priority in matter of allocation of funds. So the librarian has to muster strength and acquire necessary skill and tact for securing adequate funds. He has to convince the authorities about the usefulness of the service rendered by libraries. This can be achieved only if he advances tangible and plausible reasons for each of his demands. The authorities can be convinced easily by statistical data. So the librarian should maintain proper statistics of income and expenditure of his library. He should ensure proper utilization of fiscal grants without any avoidable wastage.

PRINCIPLES OF MANAGEMENT

Principles of Management are generalization based on experience and careful analysis of case studies. These are universally applicable. These are not rigid; change in circumstances would require adoption of these. Principles of management are a powerful tool in the hands of a manager but these must be used rather carefully after analysis of the problem and its diagnosis. Good management can be learned only through practice and by solving problem rather than by memorization of principles which may have only limited relevance to actual problem.

Henri Fayol was the first to put forward a list of general administrative principles. On the whole, his observations are valid, even today. Fayol used scientific approach. Fayol formulated the following fourteen management principles. These are the first categorized on management and these have not lost their relevance in modern management policy. These are the basic management principles.

1. Division of Work : In any organization the division of work, duties, and activities is a must. The division of work lead to specialization. If possible only that work should be assigned to a person in which field he has specialization. The principles of division of work are based on common principle of experience that every person cannot do every job.

2. Authority and Responsibility : An individual should be given authority equal to his responsibility. Possession of authority means responsibility for actions. Actual work in the library may be done by different persons but the ultimate responsibilities lie with the chief librarian. The responsibilities without authority will lead to lack of confidence.

3. Discipline : Discipline encompasses regularity, behaviors, conduct and interpersonal relationship among the staff workers. In the best interest of the organization there should be complete obedience, diligence, energy and outward marks respect. This is equally applicable to everybody.

4. Unity of Command : An organizational structure should be such that each employee is supervised by only one supervisor. An employee should be responsible to and also receive orders from only one superior. The command should generally come from the immediate superior.

5. Unity of Direction : In a planned administrative setup, direction should come from one end and one person should be responsible for similar type of jobs.

6. Subordination of Individual's Interest to General Interest : Where there is a conflict of general interest with individual interest, general interest should get the priority over the individual interest. It is desirable in any social order.

7. Remuneration : Remuneration should be reasonable and should commensurate to the qualification, experience, technical knowledge, seniority, performance and such other factors. Employees should be given incentives for successful efforts.

8. Centralization : There should be judicious distribution of work of the library in terms of centralization and decentralization. Anything that increases the importance of the role of a subordinate should be decentralized. On the other hand anything that decreases the importance of the role of a subordinate should be centralized. For example book selection and managerial function should be decentralized because in case of book selection the heads of the departmental libraries knows more about their field of specialization. But ordering should be centralized so that there is no duplication of bibliographical tool.

9. Scalar Chain : This refers to hierarchy. A hierarchy consists of a series of steps extended in an unbroken line from the chief librarian to the lowest employee. This principal implies that authority and responsibility should flow in a clear, unbroken line from the highest executive to the lowest rank. Orders go down the line traveling from top to bottom. However, information and appeal travel in the reverse direction.

10. Orders : Orders indicate the disciplined flow of discharging the respective duties and the systematic organization of work flow. It refers to the best possible management to achieve the most efficient operation of the organization.

11. Equity : In dealing with employees treatment of equality must be put into practice. Justice must be combined with friendliness and kindness by those in the executive towards staff.

12. Stability of Tenure of Personnel : Stability of tenure indicates a longer service period of an employees and uninterrupted working period. It assures better service, steady growth and systematic planning of work schedules. Rapid turnover of staff can cause anxiety.

13. Initiative : One should not only do his job assigned to him, but he should feel inspired to perform his duties. In working situation anybody may have suggestion for improvement and better work or redesigning the works schedule for better result, all the suggestion should be taken with trust by the management. Due attention, proper consideration should be given to them. This will inspire the person working with incentives and ultimately institution will get better result.

14. Esprit de Corps : The management should create environment which leads to harmony and unity. The entire employees should not feel as an assemblage of individuals but recognize their identity with the institution. Thus a sense of co-operation, a sense of belonging, a feeling of identification with the institution, a corporate sense over self, a team spirit, a feeling of unity make the institution as a organic whole.

Henri Fayol's 14 Principles and their Implication in Today's Library & Information Centres (LICs)

Principles	Fayol's Proposition	Its Implications for LIC Managers
01	Division of work by specialization	The job schedule of staff should not be rigid or static. In addition to their core or primary duties, staff should be able to perform other tasks within the organization.
02	Centralize the organizations of power	Power and authority in any organization should be decentralized without undermining corporate cohesion. This will encourage the creation of new ideas and the harnessing of staff creativity.
03	Formal system of control over staff	The various informal groups within the workplace should be strengthened. For instance, trade unions and other staff groups can be brought on board to exert some influence and control over their members.
04	Staff report to only one head	Staff can report to more than one head and still harmonize directives to work successfully
05	One plan and one head	Multiple plans from one or more heads

	for each plan	at a time is possible in order to advance corporate objectives.
06	Organization interests first even if at the detriment of staff	The interests and welfare of the staff should not be overlooked. It is only where staff are motivated that they work whole-heartedly for the organization's interests.
07	Deserving pay system	The pay system should be structured in such a way that the remuneration for workers is strictly performance-based.
08	Top management led decision making system	Creativity should not be stifled. Staff should be emboldened to initiate and implement policies relevant to their areas of specialization.
09	Vertical hierarchy and communication	Horizontal organizational structure and communication should be encouraged to the best interests of the organization.
10	Arrangement of staff and things as suitable to management	The overall interests of the customer should be taken into consideration. Arrangement of staff and things as convenient for customers (users)
11	Fairness to staff to make them work more	Fairness to staff to give them a sense of belonging. The resultant feeling of appreciation makes them work harder
12	Recruit, train staff and encourage them to remain	Recruit self-made and experienced staff but sponsor them to on-the-job training on regular basis.
13	Top management conceive and implement new ideas	As much as possible, staff should be empowered to conceive and implement new ideas for the overall benefit of the organization.
14	Ensure high moral and unity among staff	Efforts should be made to ensure high morale and unity of purpose across various cadres of staff

SCIENTIFIC MANAGEMENT

INTRODUCTION

Scientific management involves the application of a scientific approach to managerial decision-making (consisting of-collection of data, an analysis of data and basing decisions on the outcome of such analysis) and discarding at the same time, all unscientific approaches, like – rule of the thumb, a hit or miss approach and a trial and error approach.

DEFINITION OF SCIENTIFIC MANAGEMENT

According to F W. Taylor "Scientific Management consists in knowing what you (i.e. management) want men to do exactly and seeing to it that they do it in the best and the cheapest manner."

PRINCIPLES OF SCIENTIFIC MANAGEMENT

The fundamental principles, which would support the concept and practice of scientific management, are the following:

1. Science, not the rule of the thumb.
2. Harmony, not discord.
3. Co-operation, not individualism.
4. Maximum production, in place of restricted production.
5. Development of each person to the greatest of his capabilities.
6. A more equal division of responsibility between management and workers.
7. Mental revolution on the part of management and workers.

Following is a brief comment on each of the above principles of scientific management.

1. Science, not the rule of thumb : The basic principle of scientific management is the adoption of a scientific approach to managerial decision making and a complete discard of all unscientific approaches, hitherto practiced by managements.

2. Harmony, not discord : Harmony refers to the unity of action; while discord refers to differences in approach.

3. Co-operation, not individualism : Co-operation refers to working, on the part of people, towards the attainment of group objectives; while regarding their individual objectives-as subordinate to the general interest.

4. Maximum production, in place of restricted production : In Taylor's view the most dangerous evil of the industrial system was a deliberate restriction of output. As a means of promoting the prosperity of workers, management and society, this principle of scientific management emphasizes on maximizing production and not deliberately restricting it.

5. Development of each person to the greatest of his capabilities : Management must endeavor to develop people to the greatest of their capabilities to ensure maximum prosperity for both-employees and employers.

6. A more equal division of responsibility between management and workers : The principle of scientific management recommends a separation of planning from execution. According to this principle, management must be concerned with the planning of work; and workers with the execution of plans.

7. Mental revolution on the part of management and workers : According to Taylor, scientific management, in its essence, involves a complete mental revolution on the part of both sides to industry viz. workers and management (representing employers).

In fact, this principle of scientific management is the most fundamental one ensuring success of it. It is like the foundation on which the building of scientific management must be erected.

AN OUTLINE STRUCTURE OF TAYLOR'S SCIENTIFIC MANAGEMENT

Though Taylor's work and practice of it is quite comprehensive and detailed, yet the major aspects of work done by him could be summarized into the following outline structure:

1. Determination of fair day's task for each worker through scientific methods (including the best way of doing a job) : For determining a fair day's task for each worker, Taylor recommended the use of scientific methods involving the conduct of the following three types of work studies, viz.

- Time study
- Motion study
- Fatigue study

2. Scientific selection and training of workers : This aspect of scientific management is, in fact, the staffing angle of it. The workers, under scientific management, must be properly selected by adhering to a carefully- designed selection procedure. Further, selected workers must be imparted training in best methods of performing a job.

3. Standardization of raw materials, tools and working conditions : Raw materials, tools, machines and other facilities of work must be of a reasonably good quality; so that the quality of production is reasonable. Another variety of standardization which Taylor refers to is uniformity in providing work-facilities and work conditions to all workers, doing a similar type of job.

4. Functional Foremanship : The scheme of functional foremanship recommended by Taylor is, in fact, an introduction of managerial specialization-at the shop-level. In Taylor's view, instead of a single foreman performing all the aspects of the foremanship task, there must be a number of foremen-each concerned with only a particular aspect of foremanship. In the context of the scheme of functional foremanship, Taylor compares workers with students in a school class-room; where a student is imparted teaching in a particular subject by a specialized teacher of that subject – instead of a single teacher teaching all the subject to students.

In the scheme of functional foremanship recommended by Taylor, there is a provision for eight foremen of the following types:

1. Route Clerk : The route clerk is a foreman who would lay down the route (or journey) of raw materials from the raw-material stage to the finished product stage as passing through different processes and machines.

2. Instructions Card Clerk : The instructions card clerk is a foreman who would determine the detailed instructions for handling a job; and prepare a card containing such instructions.

3. Time and Cost-Clerk : The time and cost clerk is a foreman who would record the time taken by a worker in completing a job; and would also compile the cost of doing that job.

4. Shop Disciplinarian : The shop disciplinarian would look after the maintenance of discipline in the workshop and deal with cases of absenteeism, misbehavior and other aspects of indiscipline.

5. Gang Boss : The gang boss is the supervisor proper. He would see to it that all work-facilities are made available to workers and they start their work as per the instructions imparted to them.

6. Speed Boss : The speed boss is a foreman who would determine the optimum speed at which machines are to be operated; so that both-over speeding and under-speeding of machines are avoided. In this way, less depreciation is caused to machines; industrial accidents are averted and quality of production is also maintained.

7. Repair Boss : The repair boss is a foreman, who would look after and take care of the repairs and maintenance of machines.

8. Inspector : The inspector is a foreman who would look after the quality of production.

The following chart illustrates the functioning of the scheme of the functional foremanship:

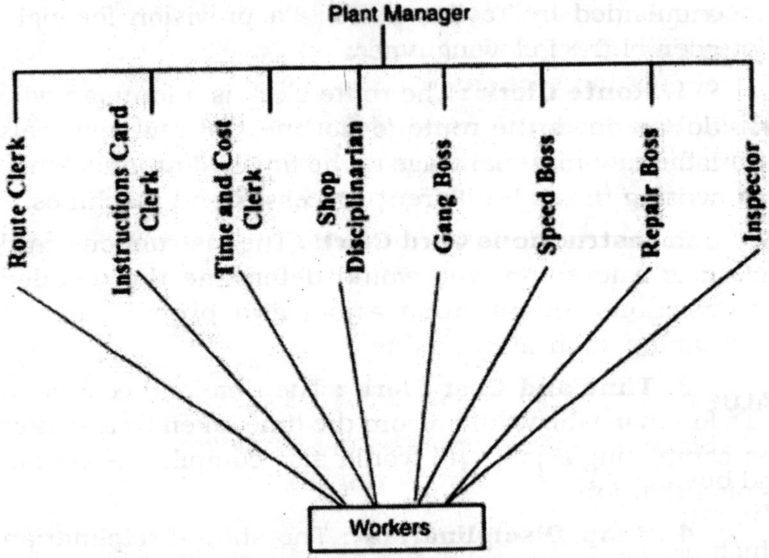

5. Differential piece-rate system of wage-payment: In order to motivate workers positively as also negatively to produce the standard output, Taylor devised a scheme of wage payment, known as the 'Differential piece-rate system of wage-payment.'

APPLICATION OF SCIENTIFIC MANAGEMENT PRINCIPLES TO LIBRARIES

The principles of scientific management can be profitably applied to the following library jobs which are amenable to proper analysis.

1. Frequently performed jobs such as duplicate checking, typing book orders, classifying, book

numbering, reproducing cards, filling cards, book charging and discharging and book shelving.

2. Repetitive jobs involving recurrence of same steps each time a job is performed, such as book charging and discharging.
3. Jobs requiring frequent movement of people or equipment such as physical arrangement between acquisition and technical sections, public catalogue, major bibliographical tools, reference, lending and circulation sections.
4. Jobs with bottlenecks such as delay caused in labeling or confusion in deciphering call numbers written in ink on the spines of books.
5. Jobs involving large amounts of money such as provision of reference service in a large library. Job-costing or cost accounting is very useful in such a case.

VALUE OF SCIENTIFIC MANAGEMENT IN LIBRARIES

Scientific management is not confined to industry and business alone. Rather it can be profitably made use of in public enterprises, nay, even in public services also, which do not have a profit motive. The main advantages to libraries which partake the nature of a public service department may be as under.

1. It helps in developing a factual data and argument. A library has an onus to satisfy the tax-payer by providing him the maximum return for each rupee paid by him for library purposes. A library is a growing organism is it needs additional funds year after year. The tax-payer wants to know why the additional amount is required. Not only an ordinary tax-payer but even experienced appropriating committees are impressed by quantitative and factual justification than eulogy of librarianship. Scientific management helps a librarian develop

such a quantitative and factual argument in his favour for securing additional funds.

2. It helps improve routine efficiency. Majority of library tasks are of repetitive and mechanical nature and are amenable to quantitative analysis. These processes include ordering, cataloguing, card filing, binding, circulation and book shelving. Scientific management can enhance routine efficiency.
3. It is a useful tool of library personnel management and financial administration. Scientific management provides us work analysis of a job which is the key to modern job classification. As a result of this analysis, the executive officer intelligently and precisely knows what he can and should expect from a worker. This provides him a yardstick to measure the work performed by a worker.

Similarly scientific management helps an administrator run his business or organization on sound financial lines. He knows the cost of each part of a job and thus he intelligently plans and avoids wastage and increases efficiency in service, thereby providing more satisfaction to his clients.

ADMINISTRATION

INTRODUCTION

Administration is a process permeating all collective effort, be it public or private, civil or military, large scale otherwise, and is that of universal nature. It is a corporative effort, directed towards the realization of a consciously laid down objectives. Since administration permeates all planned human activities, hence, it is at the center of all human affairs. Its principle aspects are formulation of policy and its implementation for the attainment in an optimum manner of stated ends in the shape of service or products. Administration is an activity which demands correct analysis and accurate orientation.

MEANING OF ADMINISTRATION

The word "administer" is derived from the Latin word "ad + ministraire" which means "To care for" or "To look after people" or "To manage affaires". Administration generally means the art to get the things done by a group of people working together in an organization, to achieve the desired objectives of the organization.

DEFINITIONS OF ADMINISTRATION

According to Goel, "Administration may be defined as the management of affairs with the use of well thought out principles, practices and rationalized techniques to achieve certain objectives".

According to Luther Gullick, "Administration has to do with getting things done, with the accomplishment of defined objectives".

According to Pfiffner and Presthus, "Administration is an organization and direction of human and material resources to achieve desired ends".

According to Herbert A Simon, "Administration is the activities of groups cooperating to accomplish common goals".

To sum up the administration is the organization and direction of human and material resources to achieve desired ends.

PHILOSOPHY OF ADMINISTRATION

Administration is a moral act and also a moral agent. The philosophy underlying the whole field of administration, particularly as it applies to library work, is based on the following key points. Administration believes in:

- Cost-effectiveness
- Execution and control of work plans
- Delegation of responsibility and authority
- Human relations and good morale

- Effective communication
- Flexibility in certain situations

SCOPE OF ADMINISTRATION

The scope of administration is very wide. It is not only restricted to public administration that deals with three functionaries, i.e. legislative, executive and judiciary. As administration is universal in nature, its scope is wide. It cover all the areas like school, college, library, business etc, all the managerial activities and functional areas of management and administration like personnel, financial, material and production are covered. In fact, it is considered as a process of planning, staffing, organizing, coordinating and controlling the resources available to get the things done or to accomplish the goals, then it can be applicable in any of the institution public or private.

IMPORTANCE OF ADMINISTRATION

- It is life blood of organization.
- It is shoulder of an organization.
- Its main function is to achieve the objectives.
- Without good administration, organization is a house built on sand or castle in the air.
- There is no substitute of good administration.
- Good administration brings out the organizational growth by effective and efficient performance.
- Good administration brings team together to work.
- It gives new ideas, through imagination, vision to an organization.
- It is considered as a brain of organization.

NATURE OF ADMINISTRATION

Administration process is intellectual, social, dynamic and creative and continuous. In fact it is multidimensional.

1. It is universal : The principal of administration are applicable in all types of set up, in every organization for their effective achievement of goals.

2. It is holistic : The whole process of administration embraces the organization and its functions.

3. It is intangible : The administration is visualized in abstract but its concepts are applicable in smooth running of organization.

4. It is continuous and ongoing process : The cycle of administration is continuous.

5. It is based on objectives : Administration is basically for the achievement of organizational objectives by utilizing the resources effectively, hence it is goal oriented.

6. It is social and human : In administration, all the efforts are directed towards the achievement of common goals. It is the environment which is important to bring the team effort and pool the potentials of all to meet the objectives of the organization.

7. It is dynamic : The administration is not rigid though work under rules, regulation to maintain discipline. But it has flexibility according to the needs and demands of a situation.

8. It is creative or innovative : Administration provides a great scope to invite the creative idea to bring about the changes in the organization.

DIFFERENCE BETWEEN MANAGEMENT AND ADMINISTRATION

Sr. No	Bases	Management	Administration
01	**Main focus**	Getting the work done	Formulation of policies, objectives, plans, programmes
02	**Function**	Execution of decisions	Decision making
03	**Concern**	Implementation of policies laid down by administration	Determination of major policies
04	**Authority**	Operational authority to implement administrative decisions	Authority to take up strategic and policy decisions.
05	Level in the organization	Applicable at lower levels of management	Refers to higher levels of management
06	Decision making	Decision is made who will execute the policies etc.	Determine what is to be done and when it is to be done
07	Applica-bility	Applicable in private sector	Applicable in government sectors
08	Directive activities	Concerned with direction of human efforts at the operational level	Not directly concerned with operational level officials

SIGNIFICANCE OF LIBRARY ADMINISTRATION

- To increase the quality assurance in library practice.
- To maintain standards in library practice.
- To develop the library staff through supervision, leadership and motivation.
- To develop administrative functions such as planning, organization, staffing, directing, coordination, recording, reporting and budgeting in the library professional practice.
- To develop strategies for the library personnel development among library through in-service education and continuing education.

- Library administrator is a person who is charged with various responsibilities ranging from administration of the staff, financial decision making and policy making for library personnel in an organization. a library administrator also has to supervise library staff, establish work schedules, manage resources to ensure quality students.

REFERENCES

1. *http://www.whatishumanresource.com/management-definitions-by-great-management -scholars.*

Unit II

MANAGEMENT PROCESS

- ***Planning** : Introduction, Definition, Components of Planning, Purpose, Classification, Characteristics, Basic Principles of Planning, Types, Advantages, Limitations, Step of Planning in Library, Planning in Library Management.*
- ***Staffing** : Introduction, Definition, Nature of Staffing Function, Steps Involved in Staffing, Need, Importance, Factors, Role of Library Manager in Staffing.*
- ***HRM** : Introduction, Concept of HRM, Definitions, Nature, Scope, Objectives, Functions, HRM-Key Responsibilities, Process.*
- ***Recruitment** : Introduction, Definition, Importance, Purpose, Needs, Process, Sources, Advantages of Recruitment through Internal Sources, Methods, Policy.*
- ***Selection** : Introduction, Meaning of Selection, Definition, Significance of Selection, Steps, Approval by the appropriate authority and issuing of appointment letter, Difference between recruitment and selection.*
- ***Job Analysis** : Introduction, Concepts, Job, Meaning of Job Analysis, Definition, Types, Methods, Purpose, Process.*
- ***Job Description** : Introduction, Definition, Roles and Responsibilities, Purposes of Job description in library, General and Specific Purpose, Limitations, Job Content/Writing Job description, Steps, Principles.*
- ***Job Evaluation** : Introduction, Meaning of Job Evaluation, Definition, Process, Objectives, Method, Principles, Limitations.*
- ***Performance Appraisal** : Introduction, Meaning, Definition, Characteristics, Objectives, Advantages.*
- ***Training and Development** : Introduction, Meaning of Training, Meaning of Development, Concept of Training and Development, Definition of Training, Definition of Training and Development, Importance, Reasons to go for Training and Development, Need, HR Role, Objectives, Difference between Training and Development, Traditional and Modern Approach, Methods.*

MANAGEMENT PROCESS

PLANNING

INTRODUCTION

A plan is typically any procedure used to achieve an objective. It is a set of intended actions, through which one expects to achieve a goal. Planning is a systematic process of deciding in what respect the future should be better.

Planning means looking ahead and chalking out future courses of action to be followed. It is a systematic activity which determines when, how and who is going to perform a specific job. Planning is a detailed programme regarding future course of action. It is rightly said "well plan is half done". Therefore planning takes into consideration available and prospective human and physical resources of the organization so as to get effective co-ordination, Contribution and perfect adjustment. It is the basic management function which includes formulation of one or more detailed plans to achieve optimum balance of needs of demands with the available resources.

Planning is the foremost element of administration which is an important tool in the hands of manager with which the course of action for future is determined. It is a decision in advance what to do, when to do, how to do and what will be the consequences. A planned layout forsees the opportunities and devises the methods and means to take advantages from these. Planning is a process which involves 'thinking before doing'. Other elements of administration can only be undertaken after planning. Proper planning can reduce the risk for loss in any task is for seen by the manager's priory.

DEFINITIONS

According to Koontz and O'Donell, "Planning is deciding in advance what to do, how to do and who is to do it. Planning the gap between where we are, where we want to go. It makes possible things to occur which would not otherwise occur".

According to Haynes and Prassic, "Planning is that function of manager in which he decides in advance what he will do. It is a decision making process of a special kind, its essence is futurity.

According to George Tarry, "Planning is selecting and relating the facts, making and using of assumptions regarding the future in the visualization and formulation proposed activities believed necessary to achieve desired results".

According to Urwick, "Planning is a mental predisposition to do things in orderly way, to think before acting and to act in the light of facts rather than guesses".

COMPONENTS OF PLANNING

There are one time use plans which can't be used repeatedly and these are known as single use plans, i.e. programmes and budgets because these once achieved, have to be formulated again. Other plans are standing plans, which are repetitively used for a long period i.e. objectives, policies, strategies, rules and procedures etc. These are enlisted under components of planning which are described below:

1. Purpose : The purpose identifies the basic function of the enterprise. For any organization, there must be a purpose which is assigned to every organization by the society. The purpose indicates exactly what activities the organization intends to engage to engage in present and in future.

2. Objectives : Objectives are the ends or goals set by the top level mangers and every activity or task of the enterprise is intended towards accomplishing these objectives. Objectives have great influence on the organizational functioning. Objectives are related to the future and are an essential part of the planning process.

3. Policies : Policies are general broad statements which provide guidance in decision making in the organization. Policies are standing plans which provide guidance to management towards executive functions. Policies define boundaries within which decisions can be made and are discretion and initiatives, but with units (Koontz and Weihrich).

4. Strategies : These are the grand plans formed in regard to what is believed. Strategy is a comprehensive and integrated plan designed to assure that organizational objectives are accomplished. Strategies help in determining a picture of the kind of organization that is envisaged. Strategies provide framework for guiding and thinking for managers and action for the executives.

5. Procedures : These are comprehensive details of actions or the guidelines for the achievement of organizational goals. Procedures give a detailed description of how the things are to be done. Procedures determine the policy of responsibility and accountability.

6. Programs : A programs is a sequence of tasks designed to implement policies and accomplish objectives. Programs help to meet a particular situation or a particular objective. "Programs are complex of goals, policies, procedures, rules, tasks, assignments, steps to be taken, resources to be employed and other elements necessary to carryout given course of action" (Koontz and O'Donnell).

7. Rules : Rules are made by management in regard to what is to be done and what should not be done in particular situation. A rule may or not be the part of the procedure but it provides better control over the situation. Rules prescribe limits of acceptable behavior of the staff working in the employees. Rules should not bring resentment to the workers but should be put in a nice way to guide them in desired direction.

8. Budget : Budget is a financial aspect which helps in execution of organizational plans in monetary terms. According to one institute, "A budget is a financial statement and quantitative statement prepared prior to a defined period of time, of the policy to be pursued during that period for the purpose of attaining a given objective. Budget is required to formulate future policies so to must be based on the past figures. It should be flexible as per the changing needs of the organization and needs to be revised time to time. Budget making improves efficiency of work, helps in bringing co-ordination and helps to uplift economy.

PURPOSE OF PLANNING

1. Orderliness : Planning helps bring orderliness and increases organizational efficiency and making work more systematic which eventually leads to saving time, economy and energy.

2. To minimize uncertainty : In big organizations, the environment is so dynamic and there is a probability of numerous possible changes. Therefore managers should have a constant eye on the development of the organization and plan further activities well in advance to avoid loss due to uncertainty. Even if the future is certain and changes are discernible, the manager involves himself in some sort of planning by way of evaluating and selecting the most promising courses of action.

3. Planning brings great economy in tasks : Course of action planned by manager focuses on the present objectives of the organization and tier attainment in least possible cost of money, material and manpower and hence helps in bringing great economy to the organizational tasks.

4. Planning brings better control : There is a better control over a planned situation as the manager can monitor and control that situation well. Thus planning helps the manager to evaluate performance by providing him the yardstick by which he can measure it and take timely and correct action for a better control.

CLASSIFICATION OF PLANNING

These are enlisted under classification of planning which are described below:

1. Structured and formal plans : Used by multiple people, are more likely to occur in projects, diplomacy, careers, economic development, military campaigns, combat, or in the conduct of other business. In most cases, the absence of well-laid plan can have adverse effects i.e. a non-robust project plan can cost the organization time and money.

2. Informal or ad-hoc plans : Are created by individuals in all of their pursuits on day-to-day basis.

CHARACTERISTICS OF PLANNING

1. Primacy of planning : Planning is a prime element of administration. Other functions like organizing, staffing, directing, controlling, coordinating, budgeting, recording and reporting are followed by planning. Planning is the prior function. No other function can be taken over without planning, therefore it is also called essence of management.

2. Planning is an intellectual process : Planning requires intellect and mental activity of a manager who is having enough knowledge and experience of this element. Planner should have comprehensive thinking to visualize in future for the implementation of the plans. Planning puts management to action as it is not instinctive but it is a conscious intellectual process.

3. Planning is a continuous process : planning is an ongoing process. It is always tentative and subjective to revision and amendments as the new facts become known. Plans are made when the organization is to be started and also goes on when it is fully established. There are modifications in the plans in the light of constant feedback about their process. Management does not rest after making plans once, but continue to plan, to formulate new plans and to correct or modify the plans on a continuous basis.

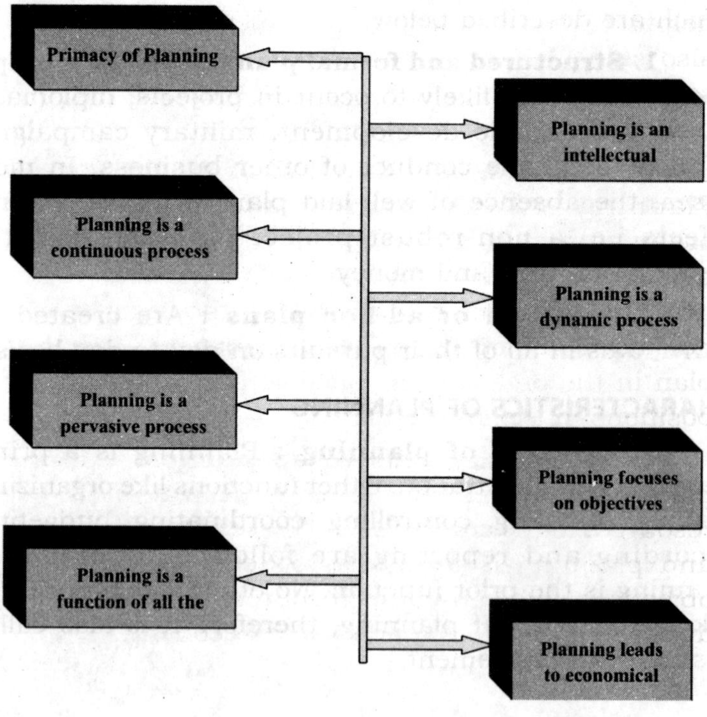

4. Planning is a dynamic process : Planning process is a dynamic process as modifications are made continuously and constantly to adapt to the changes in the environment. Planned activity does not follow a planned pattern always as there are various factors affecting the planning process and which is not under the control of administration.

5. Planning is a pervasive process : planning is not the function of one department in the organization nor it is restricted to top management. It is carried on at all the levels of management. Planning is a ubiquitous process and all the departments actively participate in the planning process.

6. Planning focuses on objectives : planning process in any organization focuses on the laid objectives to which there is differentiation in opinion of the enterprise and the techniques to achieve these. Planning proves helpful to formulate and set organizational objectives and also state the techniques to achieve them. It helps in saving time as objectives influence the course of action of future activities in an organization.

7. Planning is a function of all the managers : Planning process is undertaken by managers of organization at all levels as it is the fundamental managerial function. Planning being a pervasive process needs to involve managers from all the departments and not just confined to top level managers. All managers plan in the organization irrespective of their ranks and positions in the enterprise.

8. Planning leads to economical efficiency : planning involves the efficient utilization of various resources in the enterprise. As there are limited resources and planning is an effort to achieve organizational objectives with minimum resources. Planning prevents duplication of efforts and ensures economy.

BASIC PRINCIPLES OF PLANNING

Planning requires scientific thinking and it should spell out in clear terms the definition of the purpose, analyze the problem and make a careful and diligent search for all the facts bearing upon it. The task of planning will be well-accomplished if some fundamental principles are followed in the process. The important principles may be stated as follows:

1. Principle of Commitment : This means that certain resources must be committed or pledged for the purpose of planning. Planning is not an easy task. So, necessary help is to be taken from experts. The enterprise must be ready to exhaust the available resources for the achievement of a plan.

2. Principle of the Limiting Factor : A plan involves varied factors of different importance. This principle implies that more emphasis has to be put on that factor which is scarce or limited in supply or extremely costly. This will help in selecting the most favorable alternative.

3. Principle of Reflective Thinking : Planning, being an intellectual activity is based on rational considerations. These involve reflective thinking which signifies problem-solving thought process a process by which past experiences are superimposed on the facts of the present situation and possible future trends. None can be a planner whose mind is not active, who does not possess any deliberate power and whose sense of judgment is not strong.

4. Principle of Flexibility : Though a plan is prepared after reflective thinking, this does not mean that no departure can be made in the course of its operation. The plan should be so prepared that there is sufficient scope for changing it from time to time. Changes must necessarily be effected in the plan for taking into account new developments that may take place in the course of the operation of the plan.

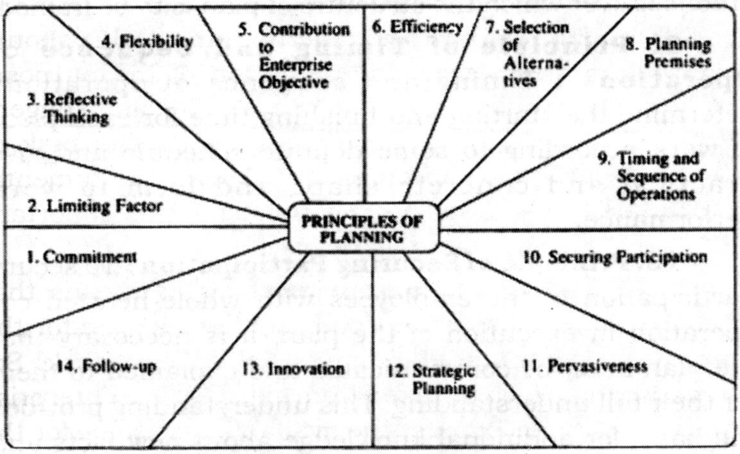

Principles of Planning

5. Principle of Contribution to Enterprise Objectives : A major plan is prepared and it is supported by many derivative plans. But all plans must contribute in a positive way towards the achievement of the enterprise objectives.

6. Principle of Efficiency : A plan should be made efficient to attain the objectives of the enterprise at the minimum cost and least effort. It must also achieve better results with the minimum of unexpected happenings. Therefore, it is to be seen that what is expected is likely to be achieved.

7. Principle of Selection of Alternatives : Planning is basically a problem of choosing. The essence of planning is the choice among alternative courses of action. There is no need for planning if there is only one way for doing something. In choosing from alternatives, the best alternative will be that which contributes most efficiently and effectively to the accomplishment of a desired goal.

8. Principle of Planning Premises : A plan is prepared against some foundations or backgrounds known as 'Planning Premises'. There must be complete agreement among the managers in respect of planning premises over which the structure of plan is to be framed.

9. Principle of Timing and Sequence of Operations : Timing and sequence of operations determine the starting and finishing time for each piece of work according to some definite schedule and give practical and concrete shape and form to work performance.

10. Principle of Securing Participation : To secure participation of the employees with whole-hearted co-operation in execution of the plan, it is necessary that the plan must be communicated and explained to them for their full understanding. This understanding provides the basis for additional knowledge about new facts and matters to the employees. This is needed for improvement in the quality of planning. It also ensures an obligation of the personnel of the enterprise to execute the plan by individual and joint participation.

11. Principle of Pervasiveness : Though major planning function is entrusted to the top management, it is not restricted to the top level only. It is a function of every manager at every level in the organization.

12. Principle of Strategic Planning : Strategic planning is essential where there is competition. It is prepared in the light of what the competitors are intending to do. Planners must take into account the strategies of the rival organisations, otherwise the planning projection may land them in trouble.

13. Principle of Innovation : A good system of planning should be responsive to the opportunities for innovation. Innovation consists in creating something new for increasing satisfaction of the consumers. This may also be stated as an important strategy of business. Innovation is a necessity for its sustaining growth in this dynamic world. Innovation is achieved through research and development and planning is required to provide such scope.

14. Principle of Follow-up : In the course of execution of a plan, certain obstacles may crop up in midway and planning may require revision, alteration or correction. This is why there must be a follow-up system in the planning process itself. This allows timely changes in the planning and makes it more effective.

TYPES OF PLANNING

Planning at various levels of organization can be classified into three types i.e. corporate planning, strategic planning and operational planning. Each type depends upon the administrative structure involved and the time taken to accomplish that plan.

1. Corporate Planning : Corporate planning is done at higher level of administration. When planning is done for the whole enterprise and includes strategies, organizational goals and policies, it is called corporate planning. Corporate planning incorporates total planning activities rather than focusing only on managerial functions. It is not bound in any set time period as it runs in the organization with other levels of planning. It includes both strategic and functional planning. But corporate planning is the starting point of planning.

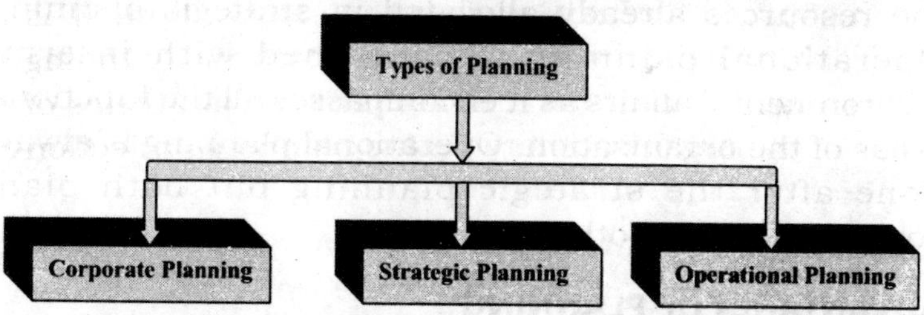

2. Strategic Planning : Strategic planning is undertaken by top level management keeping in view how to achieve organizational objectives with the available resources. In this process the top level managers set the objectives of the organization and then form a layout of plan to achieve these. This planning deals with the assessment of the enterprise including its strengths and weaknesses and how must capability is there to achieve the organizational objectives and what all resources are available at hand. Strategic planning is done due to impact of external factors i.e. the changing trends of society influenced by technological changes, economical trends, political and government policies and social changes. Strategic planning is also done to secure the resource by their proper use in day to day life. Here, the resources are procured in required quantity and time and are allocated properly for smooth organizational functioning. Strategic planning ensures success as it helps in achieving success by using the knowledge and better techniques of current information technology. Strategic planning is considered long term planning minimally done for few years.

3. Operational Planning : Operational planning is done by middle or lower level managers. These are the short term plans for a year or so forms the basis for strategic planning. In operational planning, long term plans are stated, converted in details and then implemented as action plans. This planning ensures efficient implementation of action with the proper use of the resources already allocated in strategic planning. Operational planning is concerned with internal environmental affairs as it encompasses all the functional areas of the organization. Operational planning is always done after the strategic planning but both plans complement each other.

ADVANTAGES OF PLANNING

Planning is the prime function of management and is the basis of all other functions of management. Planning is very helpful for any enterprise in following ways:

1. Attainment of objectives : Top level management form strategies and policies and fix the organizational objectives. The basic thing looked into planning is that how these objectives can be attained. In a wall defined planning the objectives are prioritized and according to that the prior objectives are focused upon primarily.

2. Better utilization of resources : To prevent the scarcity of the resources, things are planned nicely and systematically regarding adequate procurement of the resources and their proper use economically to minimize the wastage. All the resources are first planned and then, operations are planned.

3. Minimizing uncertainties : Planning is done by looking into the future which is full of uncertainties. Planning is an effort to foresee the future and hence uncertainties can be reduced by planning efficiently on the basis of decisions on past experiences and present situations. Nobody can actually prevent the unforeseen future uncertainties but these can be reduced by proper planning.

4. Better co-ordination : There are many departments in an organization, carryi8ng on with the differential functioning in their areas, so duplication of efforts is avoided by planning. Planning will lead to better co-ordination within the organization which will eventually lead to better outcomes.

5. Facilitates control : Planning helps in setting better control over the situation. Planning helps in laying down performance standards. This will enable the mangers of evaluate the performance of the subordinates time to time and if the standards are not met sometimes, remedial measures can be taken at the earliest for better outcome.

LIMITATIONS OF PLANNING

1. Time consuming process
2. Expensive
3. Requires experienced and skillful management and workforce

STEP OF PLANNING IN LIBRARY

Before actual planning, one should become aware of opportunities/problem in the light of existing situation and future possibilities. Library being a service organization, one should attempt to understand the requirement and expectations of the users. One should try to understand the present strengths and weaknesses of the library in the light of where it stands. The following steps in planning:

1. Establishment of planning objective : Planning objectives should be established for the entire organization library and then for each subordinate unit (department or section of a library). Planning objectives specifying the results expected indicate the end points of what is to be done, where the primary emphasizes is to be placed. And what is to be accomplished by the network of strategies, policies, procedures rules, and budget and programmed.

2. Establishment of planning premises : Library premises to refer to planning assumptions concerning expected internal or external environment under with plans will operate. These would consist of forecast data of factual nature.

3. Search for an examination of alternative courses of action : A number of alternative courses of action may be available, out of these through preliminary examination one should identify those which seem to promise the most fruitful possibilities.

4. Evaluations of alternative courses of action : out of the alternative appearing to be promising the most fruitful possibilities must evaluated by weighing them in the light of various library factors involve (cost, time, material, manpower, equipment etc).

5. Selection of course or course of action : At this planning the plans adopted. Incase evaluation of alternative courses of action reveals that there two or more suitable courses then the manager may take a decision to select two or more courses rather one best course.

6. Formulation of derivative plans : In the 5th step a plane was adopted in these step derivative plans almost invariable, are prepared to sport the basic plan.

7. Numbrising plan by budgeting : The final step consists of numbrising the plans by converting them to budget. Each section of a library can have its own budget, which may form part of the total budget.

PLANNING IN LIBRARY MANAGEMENT

According to Koontz and o Donnell, planning is deciding in advance what to do how to do it, when to do it and who is to do it.

1. A library operates in a complex dynamic ever changing and uncertain environment. A library being a social organization has to take care of increasing government regulations union activities and increasing community interest. A library is a growing organization and with passage of time, some of the libraries grow into large and complex organizations.

2. Planning is considered as the basic managerial function. It is one of the most important and crucial function of management. It is an essential aspect of management process at all executive levels. Planning status how the goal and/or objectives of an organization are to be accomplished. Thus it gives direction and meaning to its operations.

3. Before actual planning, one should become aware of opportunities/problem in the light of existing situation and future possibilities. Library being a service organization, one should attempt to understand the requirement and expectations of the users. One should try to understand the present strengths and weaknesses of the library in the light of where it stands.

4. Establishment of planning Establishment of planning objective Search for an examination of alternative courses of action premises Selection of course or Evaluation of alternative courses of action numbrising plan by Formulation of derivative plans course of action budgeting
5. Planning objectives should be established for the entire organization library and then for each subordinate unit (department or section of a library). Planning objectives specifying the results expected indicate the end points of what is to be done, where the primary emphasizes is to be placed. And what is to be accomplished by the network of strategies, policies, procedures rules, and budget and programmed.
6. Premises to refer to planning assumptions concerning expected internal or external environment under with plans will operate. These would consist of forecast data off actual nature.
7. A number of alternative courses of action may be available, out of these through preliminary examination one should identify those which seem to promise the most fruitful possibilities.
8. Out of the alternatives appearing to be promising the most fruitful possibilities must evaluated by weighing them in the light of various factors involve (cost, time, material, manpower, equipment, etc).
9. At this planning the planes adopted. In case evaluation of alternative courses of action reveals that there are two or more suitable courses then the manager may take a decision to select two or more courses rather one best course.
10. In the 5th step a plane was adopted in these step derivative plans almost invariable, are prepared to

sport the basic plan.

11. The final step consists of numberizing the plans by converting them¡ to budget. Each section of a library can have its own budget, which may form part of the total budget.
12. Objectives Policies Procedures Rules Programmers Budgets Grand's strategies Competitive strategies
13. Without Good planning is extremely important for any enterprise. Unrealistic planning a library would be like a rudderless ship. Can lead to a disaster and planning shortcoming can lead to failures. In order to achieve planning, some of the consideration needs to keep in view. These are given below:
    - There should be total commitment top lancing by managers as well as other from top management to supervisory level.
    - The purpose of every plan is to accomplish objectives of the organization objective should be clear verifiable and attainable.
    - It is necessary to develop a sound strategy to give direction to planning effort.
    - It is essential that every manager should attempt to establish a climate for effective planning.
    - Planning participation there should be wide participation in planning.
    - Flexibility should be in built into plans. But cost of flexibility should be weighed against its advantages.
14. Plans should be reviewed from time to time and modified if necessary in the light of change in environment.
15. Planning is considered a critical element toward the success of any enterprise. Indian libraries are at present faced with political, economic social and

ethical pressures. Prices and salary are constantly rousingly but funds being scarce, planning becomes highly a significant. In such a situation planning helps to combat the uncertainties of the future and environmental changes. It provides directions for caring out day to day operations of a library.

REFERENCES

1. Koontz, H & O'Donell, C. (1972). Principles of management: An analysis of managerial functions, McGraw Hill, 25.

STAFFING

INTRODUCTION

The managerial function of staffing involves manning the organization structure through proper and effective selection, appraisal and development of the personnel's to fill the roles assigned to the employers/ workforce. Staffing is that part of the process of management which is concerned with acquiring, developing, employing, appraising, enumerating and retaining people so that right type of people are available at right positions and at right time in the organization. In the simplest terms, staffing is 'putting people to jobs'.

DEFINITION

According to Theo Haimann, "Staffing pertains to recruitment, selection, development and compensation of subordinates."

According to McFarland, "Staffing is the function by which managers build an organization through the recruitment, selection and development of individuals as capable employees".

According to Koontz, " Staffing is defined as filling positions in the organizational structure through identifying work-force requirements including recruitment, selection, placement, promotion, appraised straining people".

NATURE OF STAFFING FUNCTION

1. Staffing is an important managerial function : Staffing function is the most important managerial act along with planning, organizing, directing and controlling. The operations of these four functions depend upon the manpower which is available through staffing function.

2. Staffing is a pervasive activity : As staffing function is carried out by all mangers and in all types of concerns where business activities are carried out.

3. Staffing is a continuous activity : This is because staffing function continues throughout the life of an organization due to the transfers and promotions that take place.

4. The basis of staffing function is efficient management of personnel's : Human resources can be efficiently managed by a system or proper procedure, that is, recruitment, selection, placement, training and development, providing remuneration, etc.

5. Staffing helps in placing right men at the right job : It can be done effectively through proper recruitment procedures and then finally selecting the most suitable candidate as per the job requirements.

6. Staffing is performed by all managers : depending upon the nature of business, size of the company, qualifications and skills of managers etc. In small companies, the top management generally performs this function. In medium and small scale enterprise, it is performed especially by the personnel department of that concern.

STEPS INVOLVED IN STAFFING

1. Manpower requirements : The very first step in staffing is to plan the manpower inventory required by a concern in order to match them with the job requirements and demands. Therefore, it involves forecasting and determining the future manpower needs of the concern.

2. Recruitment : Once the requirements are notified, the concern invites and solicits applications according to the invitations made to the desirable candidates.

3. Selection : This is the screening step of staffing in which the solicited applications are screened out and suitable candidates are appointed as per the requirements.

4. Orientation and Placement : Once screening takes place, the appointed candidates are made familiar to the work units and work environment through the orientation programmes. Placement takes place by putting right man on the right job.

5. Training and Development : Training is a part of incentives given to the workers in order to develop and grow them within the concern. Training is generally given according to the nature of activities and scope of expansion in it. Along with it, the workers are developed by providing them extra benefits of in depth knowledge of their functional areas. Development also includes giving them key and important jobs as a test or examination in order to analyse their performances.

6. Remuneration : It is a kind of compensation provided monetarily to the employees for their work performances. This is given according to the nature of job- skilled or unskilled, physical or mental, etc. Remuneration forms an important monetary incentive for the employees.

7. Performance Evaluation : In order to keep a track or record of the behaviour, attitudes as well as opinions of the workers towards their jobs. For this regular assessment is done to evaluate and supervise different work units in a concern. It is basically concerning to know the development cycle and growth patterns of the employees in a concern.

8. Promotion and transfer : Promotion is said to be a non- monetary incentive in which the worker is shifted from a higher job demanding bigger responsibilities as well as shifting the workers and transferring them to different work units and branches of the same organization.

NEED OF STAFFING

1. To fill organizational positions.
2. Ensuring job satisfaction among the personnel.
3. Optimal utilization of manpower.
4. Manpower development and advancement for taking up higher responsibility jobs.
5. Retaining personnel in the organization.
6. Developing competencies among the personnel.

IMPORTANCE OF STAFFING

The main advantages of staffing are filling the organizational positions, developing competencies to challenges, retraining personnel – professionals and optimum utilization of the human resources.

Staffing is also essential for the following reasons:

1. Key to other managerial functions : Staffing function is very closely related to other managerial areas of the business. It greatly influences the direction and control in the organization. The effectiveness of other managerial functions depends on the effectiveness of the staffing function.

2. Building healthy human relationships : Staffing function helps to build proper human relationships in the organization. Human relations are the key to better communication and co-ordination of managerial efforts in an organization.

3. Human resources development : Skilled and experienced staff is the best asset of a business concern. The staffing function helps developing this asset for the business. It inculcates the corporate culture into the staff which in turn ensures smooth functioning of all the managerial aspects of the business.

4. Long term effect : Staffing decisions have long term effect on the efficiency of any organization. Qualified efficient and well motivated staff is an asset to the organization. Staffing function assumes special significance in the context of globalization which demands high degree of efficiency in maintaining competitiveness.

5. Potential contribution : Staff selection should be based on the ability of the prospective employees to meet the future challenges that the organization needs to address. Therefore the potential contribution of the staff in their anticipated future roles should also be taken into account in staff selection.

STAFFING FACTORS

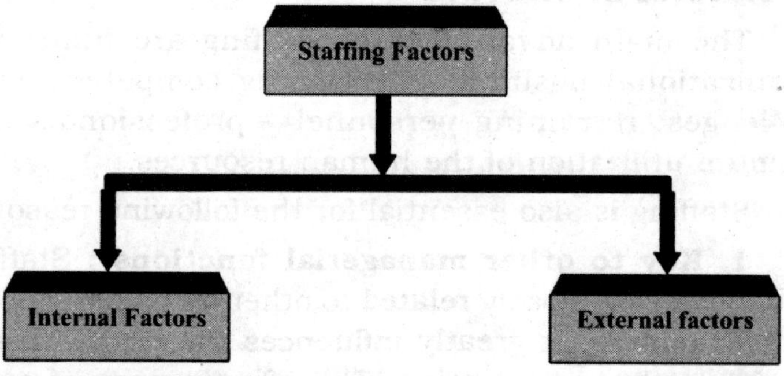

INTERNAL FACTORS

1. Organizational tasks : The staffing pattern of an organization highly depends upon the organizational goals which decide the strength of manpower, type of personnel, their qualification and skills etc. Manpower should be planned in such a way so that it has a clear focus on meeting the goals of organization.

2. Technology : The organization with staff having adequate technical knowledge and skills is demand of time in organization. As there is increase in technology with scientific advancement, the staff should make a pace with technology to bring better output.

3. Types of personnel employed : Personnel working in the organization form the organizational climate. Knowledge and skilled workers bring productivity if work with constant dedication and motivation.

4. Reward system : Reward system in monetary or non monetary terms is a source of motivation for the staff. If the reward system in the organization is well formalized, it brings better productivity.

5. Personnel policies : personnel policies including staff development and welfare do influence staffing. If the staff is provided with better provisions, it may help in retaining the staff in the organization.

EXTERNAL FACTORS

1. Educational level : Qualification of the personnel should be adequate enough to meet the demands of the job. One should meet the requirements in education, so as to avail the opportunity for job.

2. Managerial adequacy : If the demand and supply of managers in the organization is not proper, it has a positive influence on staffing pattern. An adequate manager in a firm leads to systematic management of manpower in the organization.

3. Attitudes : Prevailing attitudes of society towards work affects staffing. Head work is always appreciated with smart work. Depending upon the nature of the job, one develops the attitude towards it.

4. Economic conditions : The economic conditions of a nation or an organization have great influence on staffing. A country's organization with good economic status can afford to have more manpower and can think of innovative ideas for growth and development.

5. Laws and regulations : There are various legal liabilities that affect staffing policy of an organization.

Other factors influencing staffing are organizational policies, wages and salaries, heath provisions, transport facilities, time pattern, working hours, working environment, staff development and welfare provisions, promotions and transfers etc.

ROLE OF LIBRARY MANAGER IN STAFFING

1. To assemble the required number and types of personnel to execute required library work. This can be done by securing for each vacant position, a pool of application that can fulfill the job's requirements. To fill each position, the library manager should solicit applicants from external and internal resources.
2. When several applications have been identified for a particular position, the library manager should measure strengths and weaknesses of each candidate with regard to skill and ability requirements of position through selection test and interview. The library manager can help in selection of the most desirable candidate for the job.
3. The library manager should organize induction training and orientation program for the newly placed staff in which job responsibilities should be clarified so as to facilitate their successful adjustment to new surroundings and circumstances.
4. Library manager should also deal with staff absenteeism which constitutes a significant loss of agency resources. The manager, who succeeds in decreasing absenteeism among subordinates, can increase staffing levels, in the unit without using extra funds.

HUMAN RESOURCE MANAGEMENT

INTRODUCTION

Human resource is a term used to describe the individuals who comprise the workforce of an organization, although it is also applied in labor economics, business sectors or even whole nation. Human resources is also the name of the function within an organization charged with the overall responsibility for implementing strategies and policies relating to the management of individuals i.e. the human resources. This function title is often abbreviated to the initials 'HR'.

Human resource management is the strategic and coherent approach to the management of an organization's most valued assets- the people working there who individually and collectively contribute to the achievement of the objectives of the business. The term HRM and HR have largely replaced the term "personnel management" as a description of the processes involved in managing people in organizations. In simple words, HRM means employing people, developing their capacities, utilizing, maintaining and compensating their services in turn with the job and organizational requirement. Let us elaborate the terms human resource management.

1. **Human** (Home - The social animal characterized by superior intelligence)
2. **Resources** (Financial, Physical, Technical and Informational etc)
3. **Management** (planning, Organizing, Leading and Controlling functions)

CONCEPT OF HRM

HRM is concerned with the human beings in an organization. "The management of man" is a very important and challenging job because of the dynamic nature of the people. No two people are similar in mental abilities, tacticians, sentiments, and behaviors; they differ widely also as a group and are subject to many varied influences. People are responsive, they feel, think and act therefore they cannot be operated like a machine or shifted and altered like template in a room layout. They therefore need a tactful handing by management personnel (Ganesan, 2014)".

HRM is the process of managing people of an organization with a human approach. Human resources approach to manpower enables the manager to view the people as an important resource. It is the approach through which organization can utilize the manpower not only for the benefits of the organization but for the growth, development and self satisfaction of the concerned people. Thus, HRM is a system that focuses on human resources development on one hand and effective management of people on the other hand so that people will enjoy human dignity in their employment.

DEFINITIONS OF HRM

There are two different definitions. The first definition of HRM is that "It is the process of managing people in organizations in a structured and thorough manner." This covers the fields of staffing (hiring people), retention of people, pay and perks setting and management, performance management, change management and taking care of exits from the company to round off the activities. This is the traditional definition of HRM which leads some experts to define it as a modem version of the Personnel Management function that was used earlier.

The second definition of HRM encompasses "The management of people in organizations from a macro perspective, i.e. managing people in the form of a collective relationship between management and employees." This approach focuses on the objectives and outcomes of the

HRM functions. It means that the HR function in contemporary organizations is concerned with the notions of people enabling, people development and a focus on making the "employment relationship" fulfilling for both the management and employees.

In simple words, Human resource management is management function that helps manager to recruit, select, train and develop organization members. Or HRM is a process of making the efficient and effective use of human resources so that the set goals are achieved.

In general terms, Human Resource Management is "concerned with the people dimension in management. Since every organization is made up of people, acquiring their services, developing their skills, motivating them to high levels of performance and ensuring that they continue to maintain their commitment to the organization are essential for achieving organizational objectives. This is true regardless of the type of organization government business, Education, Health, regression or social action."

In the words of **Dunn and Stephens 1972**, "The HRM is the process of attracting, holding and motivating all manager line and staff."

The National Institute of Personnel Management (NIPM) of India has defined human resource as "that part of management which is concerned with people at work and with their relationship within an enterprise. Its aim is to bring together and develop into an effective organization of the men and women who make up an enterprise and having regard for the well-being of the individuals and of working groups, to enable them to make their best contribution to its success."

NATURE OF HRM

HRM is a management function that helps manager's to recruit, select, train and develop members for an organization. HRM is concerned with people's dimension in organizations. The following constitute the core of HRM.

1. HRM involves the application of management functions and principles: The functions and principles are applied to acquiring, developing, maintaining and providing remuneration to employees in organization.
2. Decision relating to employees must be integrated: Decisions on different aspects of employees must be consistent with other human resource (HR) decisions.
3. Decisions made influence the effectiveness of an organization: Effectiveness of an organization will result in betterment of services to customers in the form of high quality products supplied at reasonable costs.
4. HRM Functions are not confined to business establishments only but applicable to non business organizations such as education, health care, recreation and like.
5. HRM refers to a set of programmes, functions and activities designed and carried out in order to maximize both employee as well as organizational effectiveness.

SCOPE OF HRM

The scope of HRM is indeed vast. All major activities in the working life of a worker from the time of his or her entry into an organization until he or she leaves the organizations comes under the purview of HRM. The major HRM activities include HR planning, job analysis, job design, employee hiring, employee and executive remuneration, employee motivation, employee maintenance, industrial relations and prospects of HRM. The scope of Human Resources Management extends to:

1. All the decisions, strategies, factors, principles,

operations, practices, functions, activities and methods related to the management of people as employees in any type of organization.

2. All the dimensions related to people in their employment relationships, and all the dynamics that flow from it.

The scope of HRM is really vast. All major activities n the working life of a worker from the time of his or her entry into an organization until he or she leaves it comes under the purview of HRM. American Society for Training and Development (ASTD) conducted fairly an exhaustive study in this field and identified nine broad areas of activities of HRM. These are given below:

1. Human Resource Planning.

2. Design of the Organization and Job.

3. Selection and Staffing.

4. Training and Development.

5. Organizational Development.

6. Compensation and Benefits.

7. Employee Assistance.

8. Union/Labour Relations.

9. Personnel Research and Information Systems.

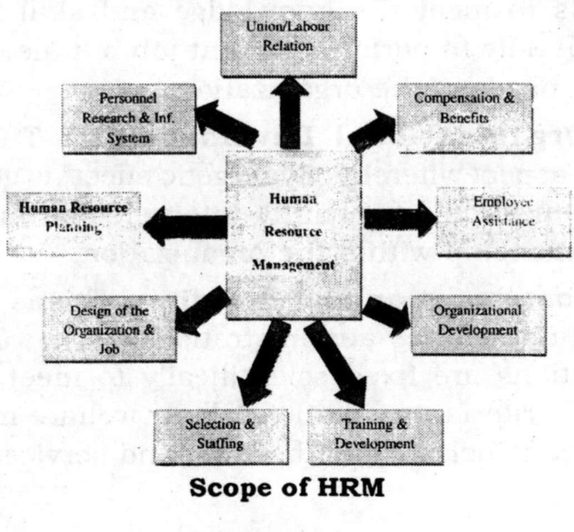

Scope of HRM

1. Human Resource Planning : The objective of HR Planning is to ensure that the organization has the right types of persons at the right time at the right place. It prepares human resources inventory with a view to assess present and future needs, availability and possible shortages in human resource. Thereupon, HR Planning forecast demand and supplies and identify sources of selection. HR Planning develops strategies both long-term and short-term, to meet the man-power requirement.

2. Design of Organization and Job : This is the task of laying down organization structure, authority, relationship and responsibilities. This will also mean definition of work contents for each position in the organization. This is done by "job description". Another important step is "Job specification". Job specification identifies the attributes of persons who will be most suitable for each job which is defined by job description.

3. Selection and Staffing : This is the process of recruitment and selection of staff. This involves matching people and their expectations with which the job specifications and career path available within the organization.

4. Training and Development : This involves an organized attempt to find out training needs of the individuals to meet the knowledge and skill which is needed not only to perform current job but also to fulfill the future needs of the organization.

5. Organizational Development : This is an important aspect whereby "Synergetic effect" is generated in an organization i.e. healthy interpersonal and inter-group relationship within the organization.

6. Compensation and Benefits : This is the area of wages and salaries administration where wages and compensations are fixed scientifically to meet fairness and equity criteria. In addition labour welfare measures are involved which include benefits and services.

7. Employee Assistance : Each employee is unique in character, personality, expectation and temperament. By and large each one of them faces problems every day. Some are personal some are official. In their case he or she remains worried. Such worries must be removed to make him or her more productive and happy.

8. Union-Labour Relations : Healthy industrial and labour relations are very important for enhancing peace and productivity in an organization. This is one of the areas of HRM.

9. Personnel Research and Information System : Knowledge on behavioral science and industrial psychology throws better insight into the workers expectations, aspirations and behaviour. Advancement of technology of product and production methods have created working environment which are much different from the past. Globalization of economy has increased competition many fold. Science of ergonomics gives better ideas of doing a work more conveniently by an employee. Thus, continuous research in HR areas is an unavoidable requirement. It must also take special care for improving exchange of information through effective communication systems on a continuous basis especially on moral and motivation.

OBJECTIVES OF HRM

HRM objectives can be summarized under four specific objectives: societal, organizational, and functional and personnel.

1. Societal Objectives : seek to ensure that the organization becomes socially responsible to the needs and challenges of the society while minimizing the negative impact of such demands upon the organization. The failure of the organizations to use their resources for the society's benefit in ethical ways may lead to restriction.

2. Organizational Objectives : it recognizes the role of HRM in bringing about organizational effectiveness.

It makes sure that HRM is not a standalone department, but rather a means to assist the organization with its primary objectives. The HR department exists to serve the rest of the organization.

3. Functional Objectives : is to maintain the department's contribution at a level appropriate to the organization's needs. Human resources are to be adjusted to suit the organization's demands. The department's value should not become too expensive at the cost of the organization it serves.

4. Personnel Objectives : it is to assist employees in achieving their personal goals, at least as far as these goals enhance the individual's contribution to the organization. Personal objectives of employees must be met if they are to be maintained, retained and motivated. Otherwise employee performance and satisfaction may decline giving rise to employee turnover.

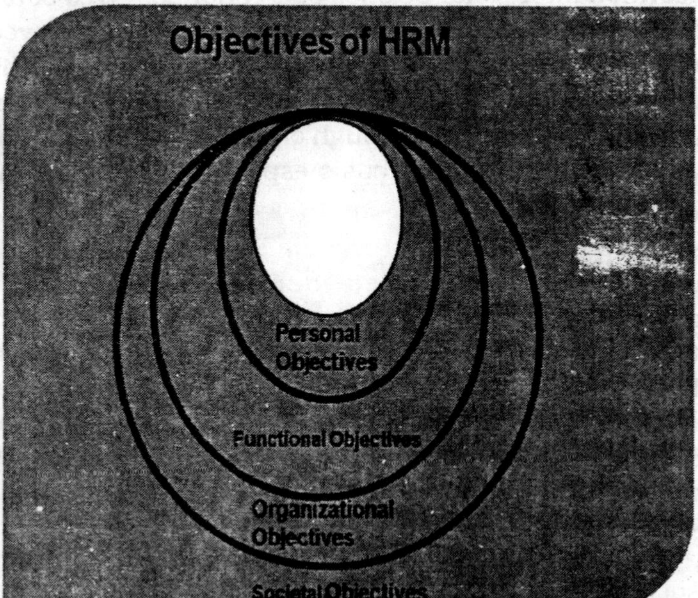

Objectives of HRM

FUNCTIONS OF HRM

Human Resources management has an important role to play in equipping organizations to meet the challenges of an expanding and increasingly competitive sector. Increase in staff numbers, contractual diversification and changes in demographic profile which compel the HR managers to reconfigure the role and significance of human resources management.

The functions are responsive to current staffing needs, but can be proactive in reshaping organizational objectives. All the functions of HRM are correlated with the core objectives of HRM. For example personal objectives are sought to be realized through functions like remuneration, assessment etc.

HR management can be thought of as seven interlinked functions taking place within organizations, as depicted in Figure below. Additionally, external forces-legal, economic, technological, global, environmental, cultural/geographic, political, and social- significantly affect how HR functions are designed, managed, and changed.

1. Strategic HR Management : As a part of maintaining organizational competitiveness, strategic planning for HR effectiveness can be increased through the use of HR metrics and HR technology. Human resource planning (HRP) function determine the number and type of employees needed to accomplish organizational goals. HRP includes creating venture teams with a balanced skill-mix, recruiting the right people, and voluntary team assignment. This function analyzes and determines personnel needs in order to create effective innovation teams. The basic HRP strategy is staffing and employee development.

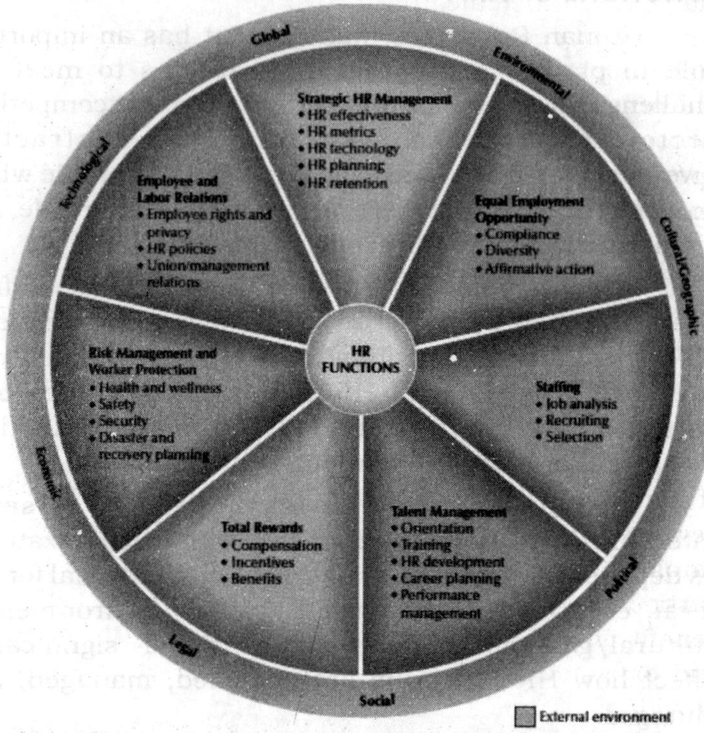

2. Equal Employment Opportunity : Compliance with equal employment opportunity (EEO) laws and regulations affects all other HR activities.

3. Staffing : The aim of staffing is to provide a sufficient supply of qualified individuals to fill jobs in an organization. Job analysis, recruitment and selection are the main functions under staffing. Workers job design and job analysis laid the foundation for staffing by identifying what diverse people do in their jobs and how they are affected by them. Job analysis is the process of describing the nature of a job and specifying the human requirements such as knowledge, skills, and experience needed to perform the job. The end result of job analysis is job description. Job description spells out work duties and activities of employees. Through HR planning, managers anticipate the future supply of and demand for employees and the nature of workforce issues, including the retention of employees. So HRP precedes the actual selection of people for organization. These factors are used when recruiting applicants for job openings. The selection process is concerned with choosing qualified individuals to fill those jobs. In the selection function, the most qualified applicants are selected for hiring from among the applicants based on the extent to which their abilities and skills are matching with the job.

4. Talent Management and Development : Beginning with the orientation of new employees, talent management and development includes different types of training. Orientation is the first step towards helping a new employee to adjust himself to the new job and the employer. It is a method to acquaint new employees with particular aspects of their new job, including pay and benefit programmes, working hours and company rules and expectations. Training and Development programs provide useful means of assuring that the employees are capable of performing their jobs at acceptable levels and also more than that. All the organizations provide training for new and in experienced employee. In addition, organization often provide both on the job and off the job training programmes for those employees whose jobs are undergoing change. Likewise, HR development and succession planning of employees and managers is necessary to prepare for future challenges. Career planning has developed as result of the desire of many employees to grow in their jobs and to advance in their career. Career planning activities include assessing an individual employee's potential for growth and advancement in the organization. Performance appraisal includes encouraging risk taking, demanding innovation, generating or adopting new tasks, peer evaluation, frequent evaluations, and auditing innovation processes.

This function monitors employee performance to ensure that it is at acceptable levels. This strategy appraises individual and team performance so that there is a link between individual innovativeness and company profitability. Which tasks should be appraised and who should assess employees' performance are also taken into account.

5. Total Rewards : Compensation in the form of pay, incentives and benefits are the rewards given to the employees for performing organizational work. Compensation management is the method for determining how much employees should be paid for performing certain jobs. Compensation affects staffing in that people are generally attracted to organizations offering a higher level of pay in exchange for the work performed. To be competitive, employers develop and refine their basic compensation systems and may use variable pay programs such as incentive rewards, promotion from within the team, recognition rewards, balancing team and individual rewards etc. This function uses rewards to motivate personnel to achieve an organization's goals of productivity, innovation and profitability. Compensation is also related to employee development in that it provides an important incentive in motivating employees to higher levels of job performance to higher paying jobs in the organization. Benefits are another form of compensation to employees other than direct pay for the work performed. Benefits include both legally required items and those offered at employer's discretion. Benefits are primarily related to the area of employee maintenance as they provide for many basic employee needs.

6. Risk Management and Worker Protection : HRM addresses various workplace risks to ensure protection of workers by meeting legal requirements and being more responsive to concerns for workplace health and safety along with disaster and recovery planning.

7. Employee and Labor Relations : The relationship between managers and their employees must be handled legally and effectively. Employer and employee rights must be addressed. It is important to develop, communicate, and update HR policies and procedures so that managers and employees alike know what is expected. In some organizations, union/management relations must be addressed as well. The term labour relation refers to the interaction with employees who are represented by a trade union. Unions are organization of employees who join together to obtain more voice in decisions affecting wages, benefits, working conditions and other aspects of employment. With regard to labour relations the major function of HR personnel includes negotiating with the unions regarding wages, service conditions and resolving disputes and grievances.

HUMAN RESOURCE MANAGEMENT-KEY RESPONSIBILITIES

Human resource management is concerned with the development of both individuals and the organization in which they operate. HRM is engaged not only in securing and developing the talents of individual workers, but also in implementing programs that enhance communication and cooperation between those individual workers in order to nurture organizational development.

The primary responsibilities associated with human resource management include:

1. Job analysis and staffing
2. Organization and utilization of work force
3. Measurement and appraisal of work force performance
4. Implementation of reward systems for employees
5. Professional development of workers
6. Maintenance of work force.

PROCESS OF HRM

1. Job analysis : The proper start to a recruitment effort is to perform a job analysis, to document the actual or intended requirement of the job to be performed. This information is captured in a job description and provides the recruitment effort with the boundaries and objectives of the search. Many times a company will have job descriptions that represent a historical collection of tasks performed in the past. These job descriptions need to be reviewed or updated prior to a recruitment effort to reflect present day requirements. Starting recruitment with an accurate job analysis and job description ensures the recruitment effort starts off on a proper track for success.

2. Sourcing

- Advertising, a common part of the recruiting process, often encompassing multiple media, such as the internet, general newspapers, job ad newspapers, professional publications, window advertisements, job centers and campus graduate recruitment programs.
- Recruiting research, which is the proactive identification of relevant talent who may not respond to job postings and other recruitment advertising methods done. This initial research for so-called passive prospects, also called name-generation, results in a list of prospects who can then be contacted to solicit interest, obtain a resume and be screened.

3. Job search engines : The emergence of meta-search engines, allow job-seekers to search across multiple websites. Some of these new search engines index and list the advertisements of traditional job boards. These sites tend to aim for providing a "one-stop shop" for job-seekers. However, there are many other job search engines which index pages solely from employers' websites, choosing to bypass traditional job board entirely.

4. Screening and selection : suitability for a job is typically assessed by looking for skills i.e. communication, professional skills, and computer skills. Qualifications may be shown through resumes, job applications, interviews, educational or professional experience, the testimony of references or in-house testing, such as for software knowledge, typing skills, numeracy and literacy through psychological tests or employment testing.

5. Onboarding : "Onboarding" is a term which describes the process of helping new employees become productive members of an organization. A well planned introduction helps new employees become fully operational quickly and is often integrated with a new company and environment.

RECRUITMENT POLICY

In today's rapidly changing business environment, a well defined recruitment policy is necessary for organization to its human resource requirements in time. Therefore, it is important to have a clear and concise recruitment policy in place, which can be executed effectively to recruit the best talent pool for the selection of the right candidate at the right place quickly.

COMPONENTS OF THE RECRUITMENT POLICY

1. The general recruitment policies and terms of the organization
2. Recruitment services of consultants
3. Recruitment of temporary employees
4. Unique recruitment situations
5. The selection process
6. The job descriptions
7. The terms and conditions of the employment.

SELECTION

Employee selection is the process of putting right men on right job. It is a procedure of matching organizational requirements with the skills and qualification of people. Effective selection can be done only when there is effective matching. By selecting best candidate for the required job, the organization will get quality performance from employees. Moreover, organization will face less of absenteeism and employee turnover problems. By selecting right candidate for the required job, organization will also save time and money. Power screening of candidates takes place during selection procedure. All the potential candidates who apply for the given job are tested.

PLACEMENT

Placement is a process of assigning a specific job to each of the selection candidates. It involves assigning a specific rank and responsibility to an individual. It implies matching the requirements of a job with qualification of the candidate.

DEPLOYMENT

The use of something or someone in an effective way. Methodical procedure of introducing an activity, process, program, or system to all applicable areas of an organization. Human resource management deals with issues related to employment deployment development of employees for ensuring the achievement of individual and organizational goals.

RETAINING

Retaining the best employees ensure customer satisfaction, satisfied coworkers product sales. Hiring and retaining good employees is one of the biggest challenges facing entrepreneurs. The task becomes all the more daunting in the absence of a brand or high revenue figures. Attracting talent is not just about getting people to work for you, it is about a long-term relationship that business grows. Therefore, it becomes more important to make hiring and retaining process a fun activity, instead of a mundane job.

PROMOTION

Promotion is the advancement of an employee's rank or position in an organizational hierarchy system. Promotion may be an employee's reward for good performance i.e. positive appraisal. Before a company promotes an employee to a particular position it ensures that the person is able to handle the added responsibilities by screening the employee with interviews and tests and giving them training or on-the-job experience. A promotion can involve advancement in terms of designation, salary and benefits and in some organizations the type of job activities may change a great deal. The opposite of a promotion is a demotion. A promotion can involve advancement in terms of designation, salary and benefits, and in some organizations the type of job activities may change a great deal.

SUPERANNUATION

An organizational pension program created by a company for the benefit of its employees, also referred to as a "company pension plan". The terms retirement plan or superannuation refer to a pension granted upon retirement. Retirement plans may be set up by employers, insurance companies, the government or other institutions such as employer associations or trade unions. All the benefits, arrears, compensations (if any), to be more precise the final settlement made financially for an employee on his retirement is known as superannuation.

TYPES OF PENSION

1. Employment-based pension (Retirement plans)
2. Social and State Pensions

REFERENCES

- Dunn, J. D & Stephens, E. C. (1972). Management of people, McGraw Hill, New York, 10.
- Ganesan, S. (2014). International journal of business and administration. Research Review, 1 (6), 147.
- Smriti, C. Human Resource Management: Meaning, Objectives, Scope and Functions.
- www.managementstudyguide.com

RECRUITMENT AND SELECTION PROCEDURE

INTRODUCTION

Recruitment is the process of having the right person, in the right place, at the right time and it is crucial to organizational performance. You'll find here information on the recruitment process, recruitment law, policy and methods, online recruitment, costs of recruitment, recruitment advertising, recruitment agencies, consultants and executive search, graduate recruitment, competency-based recruitment, application forms, curriculum vitae, and internal recruitment.

DEFINITION

According to **Flippo**, "Recruitment is the process of searching the candidates for employment and stimulating them to apply for jobs in the organization". Recruitment is the activity that links the employers and the job seekers".

According to **Yoder**, "Recruitment is a process to discover the sources of manpower to meet the requirements of staffing schedule and to employ effective measures for attracting the manpower to facilitate effective selection of able workforce".

Recruitment is the process of searching the candidates for employment and stimulating them to apply for jobs in the organisation.

To sum the recruitment is a process of finding and attracting capable applicants for employment. The process begins when new recruits are sought and ends when their applications are submitted. The result is a pool of applications from which new employees are selected.

IMPORTANCE OF RECRUITMENT

It is the process to discover sources of manpower to meet the requirement of staffing schedule and to employ effective measures for attracting that manpower in adequate numbers to faciiitate effective selection of an efficient working force. Recruitment of candidates is the function preceding the selection, which helps create a pool of prospective employees for the organisation so that the management can select the right candidate for the right job from this pool. The main objective of the recruitment process is to expedite the selection process. Recruitment is a continuous process whereby the firm attempts to develop a pool of qualified applicants for the future human resources needs even though specific vacancies do not exist. Usually, the recruitment process starts when a manger initiates an employee requisition for a specific vacancy or an anticipated vacancy.

PURPOSE OF RECRUITMENT

The recruitment process is one of the most fundamental value added HR Processes. The recruitment is especially critical for managers in the organization. The managers use the recruitment process intensively, and satisfaction with Human Resources is mostly about the satisfaction with the recruitment process. The recruitment process is sensitive to the external and internal changes, and it can be used as the best indicator for the future HR trends. By careful analysis of HR Recruitment Measures, the HR Management team can predict the trends in the job market simply.

NEEDS OF RECRUITMENT

The three types of recruitment needs is given below:

1. Planned : The needs arising from changes in organization and retirement policy.

2. Anticipated : Anticipated needs are those movements in personnel, which an organization can predict by studying trends in internal and external environment.

3. Unexpected : Resignations, deaths, accidents, illness give rise to unexpected needs.

RECRUITMENT PROCESS

The recruitment process involves a systematic procedure from searching the candidates to arranging and conducting the interviews and requires many resources and time. It has following activities as shown in figure.

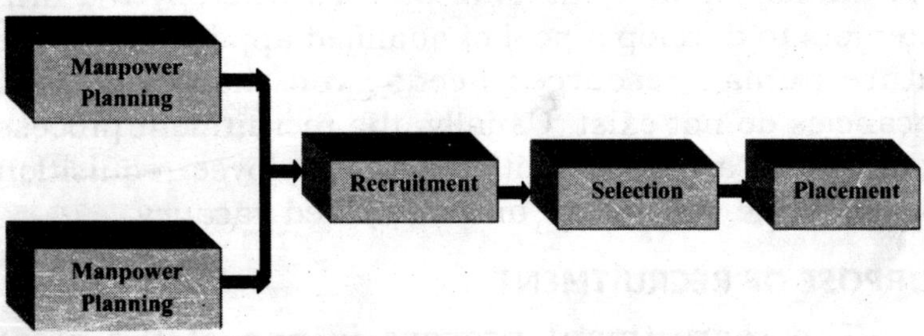

1. Identify vacancies : It beings with the human resource department receiving requisitions for requisitions for recruitment from different departments in the organization. It includes the post to be filled, number of vacancies, duties to be performed and qualification with experience.

2. Preparing job and person specification : Job specification is helpful to think of the job under broad heading: main characteristics of the training, background of the job, main responsibilities and job boundaries, expectation of job holder, resources and constraints affecting the job. It has to be decided what type of candidates is to be invited and what would be their characteristics. This need is too based on job description. Hence it is important to have job analysis, before put forward the recruitment.

3. Advertising vacancies : This is the method by which the candidate will be located it is either through internal sources or external sources and also decided the method of advertising for the post.

4. Managing response : This step is to the way adopted to receive the applications and scrutinized each application as per the requirement by the scrutiny committee.

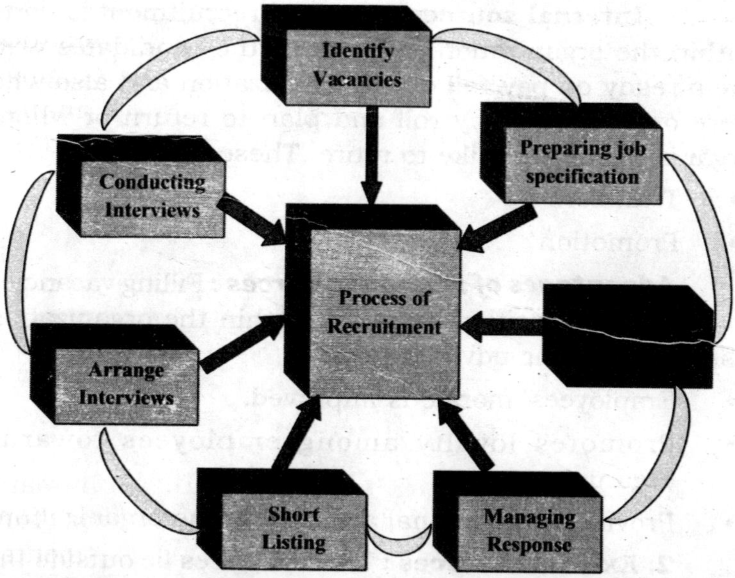

5. Short listing and identifying the prospective candidates : After the scrutiny the eligible candidates are shortlisted and a list is prepared.

6. Arranging the interview with the shortlisted candidate : Interview dates are finalized. Criteria for the merit list are prepared by the committee and candidates are informed. The selection committee is formulated.

7. Conducting the interview and decision making : Interview is conducted on the scheduled date by the selection committee, there and then the candidate are selected.

SOURCES OF RECRUITMENT

Sources of recruitment can be grouped into two categories: Internal and external sources. The internal forces or factors are the factors that can be controlled by the organization. And the external factors are those factors which cannot be controlled by the organization. The internal and external forces affect recruitment function of an organization.

1. Internal sources : Internal recruitment is done within the organization. It includes the candidates who are already on pay roll of the organization and also who were once on the pay roll and plan to return or whom organization would like to retire. These include:

- Transfers
- Promotion

Advantages of Internal Sources : Filling vacancies in the higher position in library within the organization has the following advantages:

- Employees' morale is improved.
- Promotes loyalty among employees towards organization.
- Provides promotional avenues in the organization.

2. External sources : These sources lie outside the organization. Various posts are filled from outside by present employees. Normally, following outside sources are utilized for various positions in library.

METHODS

1. Advertisement : Advertisement in leading newspaper or in professional journal is generally given search qualified and experienced personnel for vacant posts.

2. Employment agencies : Employment agencies run by the government are regarded as a good source of recruitment for bedside librarian. In some compulsory notification of vacancies to employment exchange is required by law. The employment exchanges bring employees in contact with the job seekers. There are two types of employment exchange: public and private employment exchange.

3. Deputation : This method is also quite common. The employees of one organization are selected or taken on deputation from other organization for filling the vacancies. Such employees are given choice either to return to their original organization after a certain time or to opt for the present organization.

4. On the campus recruitment : In this method a preliminary search of prospective employees is done by conducting interviews at the campus of various institutions, universities and colleges on the predetermined dates and candidate found suitable are called for further interviews at specified places.

5. Online recruitment : The job candidate sends details of vacancy on screen and asks if he or she wants to apply online. In less than a minute the candidate can send in his or her name and curriculum vitae, much faster than with earlier systems. The recruiter reviews the curriculum, vitae and decides to go ahead. The candidate clicks on the interview zone and chooses the time and place for an interview. The system tells the recruiter details of the interview. The candidate gets the reminder and can change time and place if necessary. The hiring manager can look at the candidates profile on line. More details can be built up about candidates with online tests. The candidate is interviewed and if successful clicks into offer zone, he or she will also be introduced to a mentor who will help with introducing the organization.

6. Telecasting : The practice of telecasting of vacant posts over TV (Cable and other channel) is gaining importance these days. Special programme like job watch, youth pulse, employment news etc. over the TV have become quite popular in recruitment for various types of posts.

RECRUITMENT POLICY

A well defines recruitment policy is necessary for organizations to fulfill the manpower requirements in time. There should be a clear and concise recruitment policy prepared in place, which can be executed effectively to recruit the best talent pool for the selection of the right candidate at the right place immediately. A clear and concise recruitment policy helps ensure a sound recruitment process. Recruitment policy helps ensure a sound recruitment process. Recruitment policies provide a framework for implementation of recruitment programme and specify the objectives of recruitment.

REFERENCES

- Flippo, E. B (1980). Personnel Management, McGraw Hill, New Delhi.
- http://www.recruitment.naukrihub.com/sources-of-recruitment.html.

SELECTION PROCEDURE

INTRODUCTION

Once the planning, analysis and recruitment have been conducted, the next step is selection, which is the most difficult step. Selection is an integral part of staffing, wherein one person is chosen in preference to other for the announced job position. It leads to employment of personnel. It involves a series of steps by which candidates are screened for choosing the most suitable persons for vacant posts in the organization.

MEANING OF SELECTION

Finding the interested candidates who have submitted their profiles for a particular job is the process of recruitment, and choosing the best and most suitable candidates among them is the process of selection.

DEFINITION

According to Stone, "It is a process of choosing the fit candidates or rejecting the unfit candidate or combination of both".

According to Yodar, "It refers to the negative process of eliminating of all those who appear uncompromising from all the candidates considered for possible employment".

It is a decision making process in which the management decides certain norms and principles to adhere to the standards on the basis of which a discrimination between qualified and unqualified candidates may be made.

To sum the selection is a process of differentiating between applications in order to identify those with a greater likelihood of success in the job.

SIGNIFICANCE OF SELECTION

The objective of selection process is to achieve the best fit between the job requirements and job holders. The benefits of selecting the best fit or right kind of candidates for various posts are as follows:

- Proper selection and placement of library personnel lead to build up suitable workforce.
- It helps to bring competent and skill library personnel and thereby higher efficiency in providing the quality of library.

- The satisfied library personnel with positive attitude and good aptitude will initiate to fulfill the organizational goals.
- The morale of the library personnel who are satisfied with their jobs is often high.
- There will be fewer occupational hazards and less negligence and errors if suitable library personnel are placed on various jobs.
- The selection library personnel will be more dedicated and contended towards their work.
- The quality of one's organization usually depends on its staff.

STEPS INVOLVED IN SELECTION PROCEDURE

A scientific and logical selection procedure leads to scientific selection of candidates. The criterion finalized for selecting a candidate for a particular job varies from institute to institute.

Therefore, the selection procedure followed by different organizations, many times, becomes lengthy as it is a question of getting the most suitable candidates for which various tests are to be done and interviews to be taken. The procedure for selection should be systematic so that it does not leave any scope for confusions and doubts about the choice of the selected candidate. Brief details of the various steps in selection procedure are given as follows:

1. Inviting applications : The prospective candidates from within the organization or outside the organization are called for applying for the post. Detailed job description and job specification are provided in the advertisement for the job. It attracts a large number of candidates from various areas.

2. Receiving applications : Detailed applications are collected from the candidates who provide the necessary information about personal and professional details of a person. These applications facilitate analysis and comparison of the candidates.

3. Scrutiny of applications : As the limit of the period within which the company is supposed to receive applications ends, the applications are sorted out. Incomplete applications get rejected, applicants with unmatching job specifications are also rejected.

4. Written tests : As the final list of candidates becomes ready after the scrutiny of applications, the written test is conducted. This test is conducted for understanding the technical knowledge, atti-tude and interest of the candidates. This process is useful when the number of applicants is large. Many times, a second chance is given to candidates to prove themselves by conducting another written test.

5. Psychological tests : These tests are conducted individually and they help for finding out the indi-vidual quality and skill of a person. The types of psychological tests are aptitude test, intelligence test, synthetic test and personality test.

6. Personal interview : Candidates proving them successful through tests are interviewed per-sonally. The interviewers may be individual or a panel. It generally involves officers from the top management. The candidates are asked several questions about their experience on another job, their family background, their interests, etc. They are supposed to describe their expectations from the said job. Their strengths and weaknesses are identified and noted by the interviewers which help them to take the final decision of selection.

7. Reference check : Generally, at least two references are asked for by the company from the candidate. Reference check is a type of crosscheck for the information provided by the candidate through their application form and during the interviews.

8. Medical examination : Physical strength and fitness of a candidate is must before they takes up the job. In-spite of good performance in tests and interviews, candidates can be rejected on the basis of their ill health.

9. Final selection : At this step, the candidate is given the appointment letter to join the organization on a particular date. The appointment letter specifies the post, title, salary and terms of employment. Generally, initial appointment is on probation and after specific time period it becomes permanent.

10. Placement : This is a final step. A suitable job is allocated to the appointed candidate so that they can get the whole idea about the nature of the job. They can get adjusted to the job and perform well in future with all capacities and strengths.

APPROVAL BY THE APPROPRIATE AUTHORITY AND ISSUING OF APPOINTMENT LETTER

After the candidate clears all the hurdles in the selection procedure, her or his name is recommended for selection by the selection committee and finally sent for approval to the appropriate or competent authority. When the approval is received, the selected candidates are informed by issuing his or him an appointment letter and asked to report on duty within specified date to the specified persons. The broad terms and conditions of employment, nature of job, pay scale etc. are also an integral part of the appointment letter.

DIFFERENCE BETWEEN RECRUITMENT AND SELECTION

Both recruitment and selection are the two phases of the staffing process. Recruitment being the first phase envisages taking decisions on the choice of tapping the sources. Whereas selection is the second phase which involves various activities to select the suitable candidates only. There are differences and similarities, if compare both the processes, as given below.

Sr. No	Basis	Recruitment	Selection
01	Meaning	It is a process of searching candidates for vacant posts and making them apply for the same	It is the process of selection of right types of candidates and offering them jobs
02	Objective	To attract maximum number of candidates	To choose the best candidates
03	Process	It is process of creating application post	It is process of rejecting more candidates
04	Approach	It is a positive approach	It is a negative approach
05	Sequence	It precedes selection	It follows recruitment
06	Technique	Recruitment techniques do not require high skill	It is being selection technique require highly specialized skills
07	Economy	It is an economical method	It is an expensive method
08	Time Consuming	Less time is required	More time is required
09	Outcome	Application pool-input for selection	Finalizing candidates and offering job

JOB ANALYSIS

INTRODUCTION

The concept of manpower planning or human resource planning is faced with the problem of determination of the requirement of human resources or manpower. The requirement of human resource, for the organization, is determined as a whole, both in terms of quantity as well as quality. Under the quantitative aspects, the determination of the total amount of work to be done in a particular period of time and the total number of people required to perform that work is considered; while under the qualitative aspect of human resource requirement, the type of manpower, required to perform a particular job, is considered. Job analysis is the process by which the qualitative aspect of the human resource requirement is considered.

CONCEPTS

Before we proceed to explain the concept of job analysis, let us first understand the meaning of the term 'job' itself.

JOB

In simple words, a job may be understood as a division of total work into positions.

According to Dale Yoder, "A job is a collection or aggregation of tasks, duties and responsi-bilities which as a whole, is regarded as a regular assignment to individual employees and which is different from other assignments".

MEANING OF JOB ANALYSIS

Job analysis refers to the process of collecting information about a job. In other words, Job analysis is performed upon ongoing jobs only. It contains job contents.

DEFINITION OF JOB ANALYSIS

According to Jones and Decothis, "Job analysis is the process of getting information about jobs: specially, what the worker does; how he gets it done; why he does it; skill, education and training required; relationship to other jobs, physical demands; environmental conditions".

According to Edwin B. Flippo has defined job analysis as the process of studying and collecting information relating to the operations and responsibilities of a specific job. The immediate products of this analysis are job descriptions and job specifications".

According to Herbert G. Hereman et. al., "A job is a collection of tasks that can be performed by a single employee to contribute to the production of some product or service provided by the organisation. Each job has certain ability requirements (as well as certain rewards) associated with it. Job analysis is the process used to identify these requirements".

TYPES OF JOB ANALYSIS

Two types of analysis are done: Qualitative job analysis and Quantitative job analysis.

1. Qualitative job analysis : This type of job analysis is done to gather information for personnel operations. It includes the information about duties, tasks, skills, knowledge, abilities, responsibilities, efforts, working conditions, equipments etc.

2. Quantitative job analysis : This is to develop the information for engineering purpose. The information required are duties, tasks, movements and time required.

METHODS OF JOB ANALYSIS

The information, about the duties, responsibilities and activities of a job, can be collected through a number of techniques. According to the requirements, these techniques can be used in isolation or the activities can be combined with one another. Performing job analysis is a joint effort by the HR specialist, worker, supervisor, and managers. The work of observation, analysis and developing job specification and description is performed by HR specialist, while the questionnaires are filled by the workers and supervisors. The ultimate purpose of all the job analysis methods is to develop job description and job specification. Interviews, observations, diary logs and questionnaires are among the popular methods of collecting job analysis information. However, all these methods provide realistic information about the content and human requirement of the job. The various job analysis methods are enumerated as below:

1. Personal Observation : Under this method, the job analyst watches and observes the person, performing the job, and takes notes to describe the tasks and performed duties. During a complete work cycle, various aspects, like, the tasks performed, the working conditions, the hazards involved, and the pace at which the activities are carried out etc., are observed by the job analyst. For the jobs, that involve manual/physical, standardized and short job cycle activities, this method is very much suitable. Machine operator, bus driver, flight attendant, house keeper are examples of such jobs. However, there are many aspects of a job that involve mental process and unforeseen circumstances, cannot be directly observed by this method. This method also involves personal biases, likes or dislikes, as every person has their own way of observing the things, and different people think differently and interpret the findings differently. The efficiency and effectiveness of this method depends on job analyst, whether the job analyst is skilled enough to know what to observe and how to analyze what has been observed.

Advantages

- This method provides firsthand knowledge and information about the job that is being analyzed, as compare to other method of job analysis, in which the information is obtained indirectly.
- By this method, job analyst is able to see the actual work environment, tools and equipment used, inter relationship among workers and the complexity of the job.
- This method is very simple.
- Verification of the data, collected through this method, can be done through other sources.

Disadvantages

- In the presence of an observer, the incumbent may alter their normal work behaviour, if they know that they are being observed. All this reduces the effectiveness of this method.

- For the jobs, that involves significant amount of mental efforts, this method is not very suitable.
- Job analyst may not be skilled enough to know what to observe and how to analyze what has been observed.
- This method is very time consuming.
- This method leads to personal biasness, likes or dislikes, as different people have different ways of thinking.

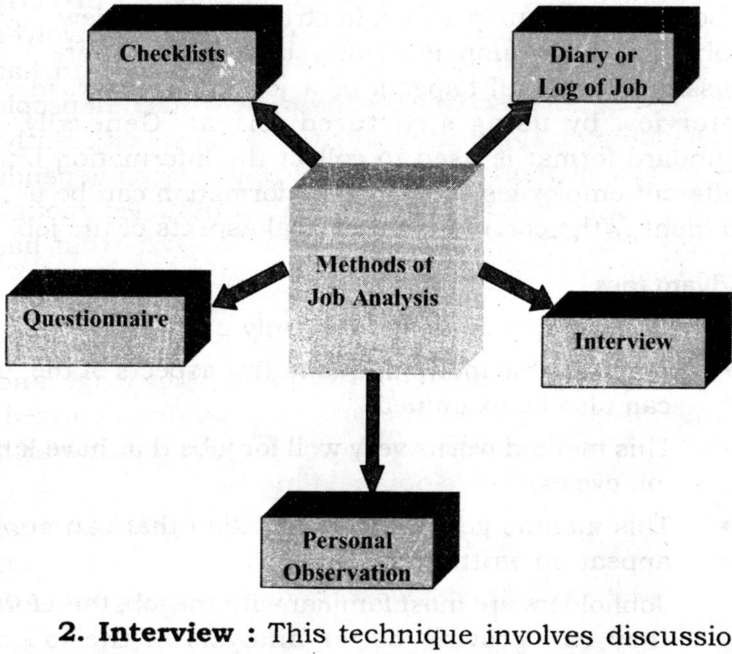

2. Interview : This technique involves discussion between job analyst and job occupants. Through this method, the occupants can come up with their own style of working, problems faced by them, use of particular skills and techniques while performing their job, and insecurities and fear about their career. This method enables the interviewer to know exactly what an employee thinks about his or her job. This method actually involves analysis of the job by the employee himself.

Interviews can be individual interview or group interview. Individual interviews are one to one basis whereas interviews with two or more occupants in a group are group interview. Interview with a small panel of experts such as, supervisors or long time employees are called technical conferences. Technical conferences reflect a census of experts thinking.

Interviews can be unstructured or structured. In unstructured interviews, the questions and the area of discussions are unspecified. In structured interview, each point for discussion is clearly laid down. There is a possibility that all aspects of a job are covered in an interview by using structured format. Generally, a standard format is used to collect the information from different employees so that the information can be used to identify the common and critical aspects of the job.

Advantages

- This method is most commonly used.
- Through this method, qualitative aspects of the job can also be examined.
- This method works very well for jobs that have long job cycles.
- This method generates information that can never appear on written format.
- Jobholders are most familiar with the job, therefore, they can provide better analysis of the job as compare to anyone else.

Disadvantages

- The efficiency of this method depends on the interviewer's ability to take interview.
- This method of job analysis may become faulty if the interviewer puts ambiguous questions to workers.
- With the purpose to add greater weight age to their

position, the workers may exaggerate their job duties.

- If a number of jobs are to be studied, then this method is very time and money consuming.
- In order to show that their job is very complex, the workers may distort information.
- If the purpose of interview is not clear, employees may provide information to protect their own interests.

3. Questionnaire : In this method of collecting job analysis information, a questionnaire is developed and given to the employees and supervisors / managers, to provide the answers. This questionnaire is related to the nature of duties, tasks and responsibilities, related to the job. The questionnaire can be of two types: structured questionnaire and unstructured questionnaire. Structured questionnaire is like checklists. Each employee gets an inventory of perhaps hundreds of specific duties or tasks. Employee is required to answer whether he or she performs each task or not, and if performs, how much time is normally spent on each one. The unstructured questionnaire is open – ended that simply asks the employees to describe the major duties of their job. The best questionnaire generally falls between the two extremes. A questionnaire is a quick and efficient method of collecting information from a large number of employees. This method is less costly as compare to the interviewing method of collecting information. But this method is expensive and time consuming.

Various organizations use standardized questionnaires that have been developed by some agency. Most of these questionnaires are of two types: (1) Position analysis questionnaire (2) Management position description questionnaire, which are discussed as follows:

Position Analysis Questionnaire : It is a structured questionnaire that is designed to collect quantitative information, about the different aspects of the job. In this method, the job and human characteristics are identified individually, and then inter relationship between them is developed, for the purpose of analysis. The PAQ covers 194 job elements that are divided into six major categories:

- Information input
- Mental processes
- Work output
- Relationship with others
- Job content
- Other job characteristics.

The job descriptors, who explain the job based elements, are rated on a scale of extent of use, importance, time, the possibility of occurrence, applicability and a special code for certain jobs. The job analyst decides what role each item plays, and to what extent. The analyst can do this online by using the site www.paq.com. The PAQ results are used to compare one job with the other, and then to assign pay levels for each job.

Management Position Description Questionnaire : Managerial jobs differ in character, from other jobs, with clearly identifiable routines and procedures. Therefore, some specialized methods have evolved for their analysis. One of widely used methods, known as management position description questionnaire, was developed by a computer company. This is a structured questionnaire, containing 208 items, related to the responsibilities, restrictions, demands, and other miscellaneous position characteristics of the managers. These 208 items have been grouped under 13 categories as:

- Product, marketing and financial strategy planning
- Coordination of other organizational units and personnel

- Internal business control
- Products and services responsibilities
- Public and customer relations
- Advanced consulting
- Autonomy of actions
- Approval of financial commitments
- Staff service
- Supervision
- Complexity and stress
- Advanced financial responsibilities
- Broad personnel responsibilities

4. Diary or Log of Job Incumbent : The daily listings, made by the workers, what they do during the day are called maintaining the dairy or log. In this technique, the workers maintain the diary, on daily basis, by recording the job duties, frequencies of the duty etc. This technique, when supplemented with subsequent interviews with the workers and the supervisors, produces the complete picture of the job.

In order to have good information about the job, the diary or log should be updated. An examination of the routineness or non-routineness of the job, duties can be made by comparing the daily, weekly or monthly figures of the dairy. Some jobs are very difficult to observe, like that of engineers, scientists, and senior executives etc. In these types of jobs, diary or log provides a useful basis for gathering information, related to the job. The problem, with this method of collecting the job related information, is that the individuals are not disciplined enough to keep such a dairy or log. But in order to avoid such pitfalls, some firms take a high-tech approach to dairy or logs. Pocket dictating machines and pagers are given to the employees. The employers page the workers at random times, during the day, who dictate what they are doing at that time.

5. Checklists : The appearance of questionnaire and checklists is similar but the checklist is more structured than a questionnaire. A checklist contains fewer subjective judgments and tends to be either yes or no variety but a questionnaire depends on the job holders to provide narrative description of the tasks, skills, knowledge, abilities, working conditions etc., involved in the performance of their job. A checklist includes a large number of activities and the job holder is required to tick only those activities that are included in their jobs. The preparation of checklists requires a lot of efforts by the specialists who prepares this list. While preparing this list, all the relevant information about the job can be collected by asking the supervisors, industrial engineers and other familiar with the work. After the preparation of the checklist it is sent to the job holder. The responses of the job holder are clustered by applying some statistical methods and then that will be the basis for tabulating job related data.

This method of collecting job related information is very useful in large firms that have a large number of employees, assigned to one particular job. This technique is amenable to tabulation and recording on electronic equipment. However, this technique is very costly and not suitable for small firms.

PURPOSE OF JOB ANALYSIS

One of the main purposes of conducting job analysis is to prepare job description and job specification which in turn helps to hire the right quality of workforce into the organization. Following are the various purpose of job analysis.

1. Manpower Planning : Job analysis data helps to forecast the library manpower required as per the knowledge and skills. It helps to determine the quality of library personnel required in the library organization.

2. Recruitment : Job analysis is used to find out

how and when to hire library personnel and which type of personnel are required.

3. Selection : It makes easy for the mangers to select the right library personnel by understanding accurately what the job is. Job analysis can be used in selection procedures to identify or develop: interview question, selection tests.

4. Placement and Induction : After selection, the library personnel are placed in different section based on the place best suited to them. If it is not sure that which type of duties are required in particular section may not be possible to place the right person at right place. Similarly, effective job orientation cannot be delivered without understanding of the needs of each job.

5. Determining training needs : Job analysis can be used in training needs assessment. It also helps to identify or develop training content, assessment tests to measure effectiveness of training, equipment to be used in delivering the training, methods of training.

6. Compensation : Job analysis can be used in compensation to identify or determine: skill levels, compensable job factors, work environment, responsibilities and required level of education.

7. Counseling : It is very important that if the library managers know about the jobs, can counsel the employees for their career. This is possible by job analysis.

8. Employee Safety : By doing the job analysis, the information regarding the working conditions and unsafe practice will also be revealed that help the library managers to improve upon on those things.

9. Performance Review : Job analysis can be used in performance review to identify or develop: goals and objectives, performance standards, evaluation criteria, length of probationary period, duties to be evaluated.

10. Job Evaluation : Job analysis helps in evaluating the worth of job, the skill and knowledge required for the particular job. This can help in standardization of work, simplification of work and proper utilization of employees.

11. Job Design and Redesign : Based on job analysis, it is easy for the library mangers to locate weak areas and they can take action to simplify certain steps and improve the existing one.

PROCESS OF JOB ANALYSIS

The major steps involved in job analysis are: organizational analysis, selection of strategic choices, collection of job analysis data, information processing, preparation of job description, preparation of job specification, depicted in figure.

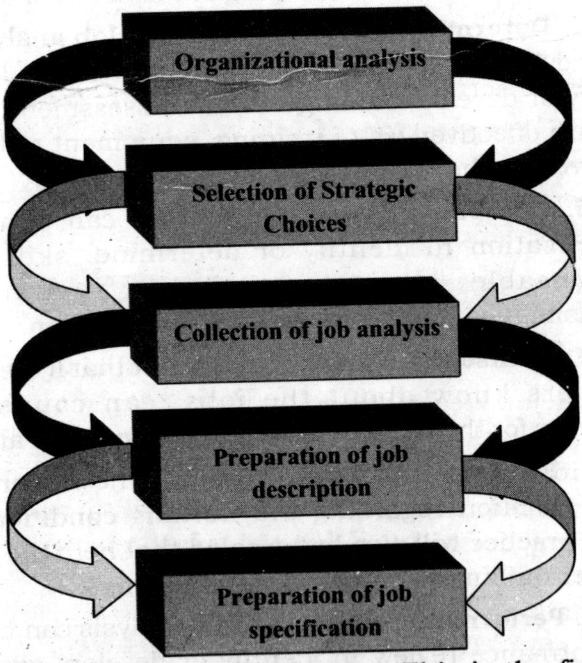

1. Organizational analysis : This is the first step to start with job analysis. Get the overall picture of various jobs in the library organization. Find out the link between jobs and organizational objectives and contribution of various jobs to the efficiency and effectiveness of the organization.

2. Selection of Strategic Choices : Decide a particular job to be selected for analysis, the level of its details, employee's involvement, timing of frequency of analysis and sources of data.

3. Collection of job analysis data and Information Processing : This step involves the collection of data on the characteristics of jobs, the required behavior and personal qualification required to carry out the job. Several methods and techniques are also available for collecting data. The collected data then analyzed or processed.

4. Preparation of job description : In this step, the contents of the job in terms of functions, duties, responsibilities, operations etc. are prepared in a particular format.

5. Preparation of job specification : This step involves describing the specification of the job including the personal attributes in terms of traits, skills, training and experience etc.

JOB DESCRIPTION

INTRODUCTION

A job description identifies essential and non-essential tasks that are assigned to a specific position. It also identifies reporting relationships and may also describe required qualifications, minimum requirements, working conditions, and desirable qualifications. Supervisors are responsible for developing and maintaining accurate and current job descriptions for their staff. The duties should be appropriate for the classification and consistent with the library specification. It is not uncommon for duty statements to vary within the same classification due to the various departmental settings and organizational structures.

The data collected through job analysis provides the basis for preparing job description and job specifications. Job description is a written description of a job and the types of duties it includes. Since there is no standard format for job descriptions, they tend to vary in appearance and content from one organization to another. However, most job descriptions will contain at least three parts: the job title, a job identification section and a job duties section. If the job specifications are not prepared as a separate document, they are usually stated in the concluding section of the job description. Highlight in HRM shows a job description for an HR employment assistant.

This sample job description includes both job duties and job specifications and should satisfy most of the job information needs of managers who must recruit, interview and orient a new employee. Job descriptions are of value to both the employees and employer. From the employee's standpoint, job descriptions can be used to help them learn their job duties and remind them of the results they are expected to achieve. From the employer's standpoint, written job descriptions can serve as a basis for minimizing the misunderstandings that occur between library managers and their subordinates concerning job requirements. They also establish management's right to take corrective action when the duties covered by the job description are not performed as required.

DEFINITION

According to Torrington, "A job description is usually developed by conducting a job analysis, which includes examining the tasks and sequences of tasks necessary to perform the job. The analysis considers the areas of knowledge and skills needed for the job. A job usually includes several roles".

According to Hall, "The job description might be

broadened to form a person specification or may be known as "Terms of Reference". The person/job specification can be presented as a stand-alone document, but in practice it is usually included within the job description. A job description is often used in recruitment".

To sum up the job description is a list that a person might use for general tasks, or functions, and responsibilities of a position. It may often include to whom the position reports, specifications such as the qualifications or skills needed by the person in the job, and a salary range. Job descriptions are usually narrative, but some may instead comprise a simple list of competencies for instance, strategic human resource planning methodologies may be used to develop a competency architecture for an organization, from which job descriptions are built as a shortlist of competencies.

ROLES AND RESPONSIBILITIES OF JOB DESCRIPTION

A job description may include relationships with other people in the organization:

- Supervisory level.
- Managerial requirements.
- Relationships with other colleagues.

PURPOSES OF JOB DESCRIPTION IN LIBRARY

- The job description help the library personnel applicant know about the duties and responsibilities with a particular job position and clarify work function.
- It facilitates the library employee to understand properly the requirements of job and gives a summary of important functions and expectations of particular job position to a potential employee.
- It aids in job evaluation.
- It provides basis for manpower planning.
- It assists in recruitment, selection, placement,

orientation, career planning and evaluation of library employee.

- It also helps in benchmarking the performance standards.
- For classifying the levels of library functions according to skill levels.
- To identify training needs of library personnel.
- Serve as a channel of communication.
- Helps in job evaluation.
- Maintaining library employee's discipline.
- Help in work scheduling.

GENERAL AND SPECIFIC PURPOSE OF JOB DESCRIPTION

Job description is all about collecting and recording basic job-related data that includes job title, job location, job summary, job duties, reporting information, working conditions, tools, machines and equipments to be used and hazards and risks involved in it. A job description may or may not have specific purpose. It depends on what HR managers want to determine and what is the objective of conducting the process of job analysis.

Job Description is a summary of job analysis findings that helps managers determine what an employee is supposed to do when onboard. The purpose of job description depends on the level of details the job findings include. Job description carried for general purpose typically involves job identification (title, designation, location) and a statement of duties and functions of a prospective or existing employee. A specifically carried job description includes detailed information about the kind of job, how it is supposed to be performed and what is expected to be delivered. Let's discuss the general and specific purpose of conducting a job description.

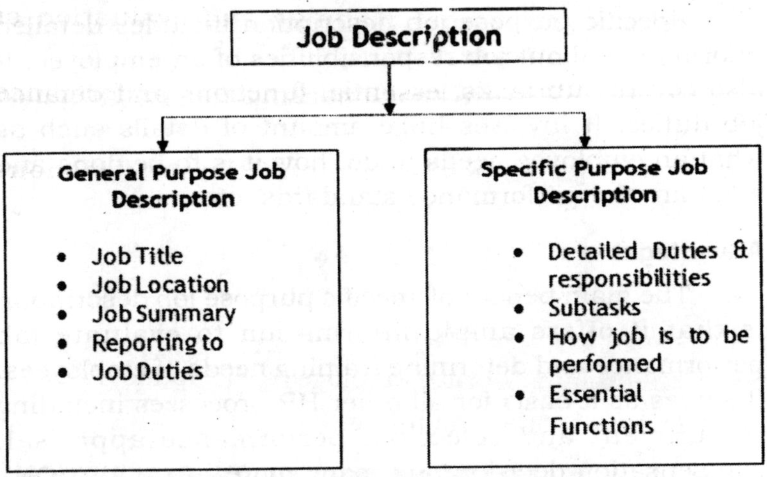

GENERAL PURPOSE OF JOB DESCRIPTION

General purpose job descriptions are used by organizations to find the very basic information about a particular job opening. Though data includes worker's duties but does not contain sub tasks, performance standards and basis for evaluating jobs and establishing right compensation packages.

Advantages

The main benefit of general purpose job description is that it does not consume much time and quickly provides basic information to managers. It does not require much human efforts and is very easy and convenient to carry out. Additionally, a job analyst does not have to conduct deep research to gather the required details.

Disadvantages

The main disadvantage of general purpose job description is that it does not provide managers with full-fledged information about job context and sub tasks. Sometimes, a manager may fail to extract correct information from such small amount of data.

SPECIFIC PURPOSE OF JOB DESCRIPTION

Specific purpose job description includes detailed information about job responsibilities of an employee. It also covers sub tasks, essential functions and detailed job duties. It involves huge amount of details such as what an employee needs to do, how it is to be done and what are the performance standards, etc.

Advantages

The main benefit of specific purpose job description is that it offers ample information to evaluate job performance and determine training needs of employees. It serves as a basis for all other HR processes including recruitment and selection, performance appraisal, compensation decision and many more.

Disadvantages

Though it assists managers in decision making process but it has its own limitations. The process, however, may take very long and consume lots of human efforts. Since, it involves collecting detailed information; the biased nature of job analyst can cause severe problems. The data collected may not be 100 percent genuine. Therefore, it can be said that information collected during job analysis defines the purpose of job description. If data collected is extremely basic, it will serve only the general purpose and therefore, cannot be used for making management decisions. On the other hand, detailed data serves the specific purpose and can be easily used while making important decisions.

LIMITATIONS OF JOB DESCRIPTION

Prescriptive job descriptions may be seen as a hindrance in certain circumstances:

- Job descriptions may not be suitable for some senior managers as they should have the freedom to take the initiative and find fruitful new directions;

- Job descriptions may be too inflexible in a rapidly changing organization, for instance in an area subject to rapid technological change;
- Other changes in job content may lead to the job description being out of date;
- The process that an organization uses to create job descriptions may not be optimal.

JOB CONTENT/WRITING JOB DESCRIPTION

A job description should be clear, concise and should be clearly communicated to every library employee. A standard format of the job description must cover the following information adequately:

1. Job title and location : It includes the title of the job/designation, department and code number.

2. Job summary : It is a brief write up about the job, its nature.

3. Job activities/duties : A description of tasks and the role needed for performing the job, facilities used.

4. Skills and specifications : The skills, qualities and other competencies required in the employee to work better and efficiently in the position.

5. Education and Qualifications : The minimum educational and professional degrees needed to make one eligible for the job category as well as must specify the other qualifications, training, certifications and experience needed.

6. Reporting relationship : Reporting relationship should be clearly indicated.

7. Extent of supervision : His/her extent of supervision available may also be stated in job description.

8. Working conditions : The physical environment, any hazards, etc

- ***Work environment*** **:** The size of work group, work culture, interpersonal interaction etc.

- ***Performance standards*** **:** The standards required for the personnel to evaluate for the performance.

STEPS TO JOB DESCRIPTION

Various steps are taken to develop job descriptions. These are:

1. Decide to whom and who is going to develop job descriptions : Usually the library managers prepare job descriptions. He/she can take help of other reporting library managers. However, the other library employees performing similar job duties contribute to the overall library department of a job description. There it is decided for whom the job description is to be prepared.

2. Performing job analysis : Do job analysis. Follow all the steps of job analysis. Decide the time, methods of gathering job data and processing of data.

3. Preparing and standardizing the job description : Prepare a rough draft. Use standardized format for writing job description. Prepare a list of job responsibilities and prefer to create the final format appropriate with job descriptions. Get it validated from the expert. Conduct a field study to standardize the job description.

4. Evaluating the job description from time to time : This is to ensure that it accurately reflects the work nature of library employee and expectations of outcomes form them.

PRINCIPLES IN PREPARING THE JOB DESCRIPTION

Following principles should be kept in mind while preparing the job description.

- It should be up to date. Make modifications if required. It must correspond accurately to current job requirements.
- Job title should indicate the nature of the work and principle demands made by the job.

- The summary of duties should be clearly specified and defined and should give an overview of what the job essentially is.
- It should be descriptive but short, but sufficiently complete, not overly detailed.
- Look at the job from all the angles. Ask others for their opinions concerning proposed job descriptions.
- Use clear and concise statements that can be understood by very one.
- Use specific terms.

REFERENCES

- Torrington & Hall. Personnel Management: A New Approach. Prentice Hall International. p. 205.

JOB EVALUATION

INTRODUCTION

The aim of job evaluation is to provide a systematic and consistent approach to defining the relative worth of jobs within a workplace, single plant or multiple site organizations. It is a process whereby jobs are placed in a rank order according to overall demands placed upon the job holder. It therefore provides a basis for a fair and orderly grading structure. Job evaluation does not determine actual pay. That is a separate operation, normally the subject of negotiation between management and employees or their trade union representatives. Only the job is evaluated, not the person doing it. It is a technique of job analysis, assessment and comparison and it is concerned with the demands of the job, such as the experience and the responsibility required carrying out the job. It is not concerned with the total volume of work, the number of people required to do it, the scheduling of work, or the ability of the job holder. Several techniques of job evaluation have developed, varying in approach. Some involve an examination of jobs according to criteria such as skill, responsibility and working conditions. Others are less complex.

MEANING OF JOB EVALUATION

Job evaluation deals with money and work. It determines the relative worth or money value of jobs.

DEFINITION

Edwin B. Flippo defines job evaluation as, "A systematic and orderly process of determining the worth of a job in relation to other jobs".

International Labour Organisation defined job evaluation as, "attempt to determine and compare demands which the normal performance of a particular job makes on normal workers without taking into account the individual abilities or performance of the workers concerned."

Wendell L. French defined job evaluation as, "a process of deter- mining the relative worth of the various jobs within the organisation, so that differential wages may be paid to jobs of different worth." Job evaluation is defined as "the overall activity if living an orderly, systematic method and procedure of ranking, grading and weighing of jobs to determine the value a specific job in other jobs."

PROCESS OF JOB EVALUATION

The process of job evaluation involves the following steps:

1. Gaining acceptance : Before undertaking job evaluation, top management must explain the aims and uses of the programme to the *employees* and *unions*. To elaborate the program further, oral presentations could be made. Letters, booklets could be used to classify all relevant aspects of the job evaluation programme.

2. Creating job evaluation committee : It is not possible for a single person to evaluate all the key jobs in an organization. Usually a job evaluation committee consisting of experienced employees, union representatives and *HR* experts is created to set the ball rolling.

3. Finding the jobs to be evaluated : Every job need not be evaluated. This may be too taxing and costly. Certain key jobs in each department may be identified. While picking up the jobs, care must be taken to ensure that they represent the type of work performed in that department.

4. Analyzing and preparing *job description* : This requires the preparation of a job description and also an analysis of job needs for successful performance.

5. Selecting the method of evaluation : The most important method of evaluating the jobs must be identified now, keeping the job factors as well as organizational demands in mind.

6. Classifying jobs : The relative worth of various jobs in an organisation may be found out after arranging jobs in order of importance using criteria such as skill requirements, experience needed, under which conditions job is performed, type of responsibilities to be shouldered, degree of *supervision* needed, the amount of *stress* caused by the job, etc. Weights can be assigned to each such factor. When we finally add all the weights, the worth of a job is determined. The points may then be converted into monetary values.

OBJECTIVES OF JOB EVALUATION

- To gather data and information relating to job description, job specification and employee specifications of various jobs in an organisation.
- To compare the duties, responsibilities and demands of job with other jobs.
- To determine the hierarchy and place of various in an organisation.

- To determine the ranks or grades of various jobs.
- To ensure fair and equitable wages on the basic of relative worth or value of jobs. In other words, equal wages are fixed to the jobs of equal worth or value.
- To minimize wage description based on sex, age, caste, region, religion etc.

METHOD OF JOB EVALUATION

Job evaluation as evident from the word itself aims at evaluating the job and not the person. It is a process of evaluating and determining the value of the job for an organization. The evaluation is always in relative and not absolute terms. The idea is evaluate a certain job against other jobs in the organization so that a fair compensation system against various bands or levels can be established. Organisations use various ways to evaluate jobs for arriving upon a compensation scheme. They vary with the size of the organisation and the kind of industry they operate in. Job ranking, pair comparison and benchmarking are the various ways of evaluation.

1. Job ranking method : This is the simplest method of evaluating jobs. In this method jobs are taken as a whole and ranked against each other. It consists of arranging job in a hierarchy of complexity from highest to lowest. A simple ranking of library jobs from positions of higher to positions to lower complexity, using job description will give hierarchy.

2. Job grading system : In this system grading of library jobs can be done based on nature of job for example: high level of administrative jobs can be labeled grade I, supervisory jobs as grade II likewise and set the appropriate pay range for each grade. This is also called job classification system.

3. Point system : this is quantitative method of job evaluation. In the point system various aspects or parts of the job such as education and experience required to perform the job are assessed and a point value is awarded as the higher the educational requirements of the job the higher the point scored.

4. Factor comparison method : It is a quantitative method of job evaluation in which each job in the library department is compared with each other, one job factor at a time. Usually factor comparison analysis is done by taking five factors: mental requirement, physical requirements, skill requirements, responsibility and working conditions. It can also be compared by taking three factor as: job knowledge, judgment and responsibility.

PRINCIPLES OF JOB EVALUATION

1. Definition : Jobs must be clearly defined such that they are identifiable and easily distinguishable. These jobs must then be part of the job description.

2. Evaluation : A job evaluation scheme must be arrived upon and used as a standard and all jobs in the organisation must be evaluated as per that scheme only.

3. Job Understanding : Job evaluators need to have deep insights into the job design process. They must have a methodical understanding of various tasks involved.

4. Concern : Job evaluation must be concerned with the job and not with the person. i.e. it is the job that has to be evaluated and not the person.

5. Assessment : The assessment has to be carried out in an acceptable manner and by competent people. Further, it is based on judgment and is not scientific but can however be used to make objective judgments if used correctly.

LIMITATIONS OF JOB EVALUATION

1. Job evaluation is not completely scientific.
2. Most of the techniques are difficult to understand, even for the supervisors.

3. The factors taken by the programme are not exhaustive.
4. There may be wide fluctuations in compensable factors in view of changes in technology, values and aspirations of employers etc.
5. Employees, trade union leaders, management and the programme operators may assign different weight to different factors, thus creating grounds for dispute.

REFERENCES

- Edwin B. Flippo, Personnel Management, Tata McGraw-Hill Publishing Company Limited, New Delhi, 1980, p. 258.
- International Labour Organization, Job evaluation–Studies and Reports, New Series, No.56, Geneva, 1960, p.8.

PERFORMANCE APPRAISAL

INTRODUCTION

Performance appraisal is assessment of how staff members are doing their job. It is a process of evaluation of the individual's performance, process in job and assessing their potential for future development. Employee performance is the product of three underlying factors, i.e. ability, motivation and environment. A defect in any of the three will impair his performance. It is quite nature for a subordinate wanting to know what his supervisor thinks of his/her work.

MEANING OF PERFORMANCE APPRAISAL

Appraisal means "estimate the value or quality" and performance appraisal means "An annual review of an employee's overall contributions to the company by his/her manager".

DEFINITION

According to Edwin Flippo, "Performance appraisal is the systematic, periodic and an impartial rating of an employee's excellence in matters pertaining to his present job and his potential for a better job.

According to Cummings, "The overall objective of performance appraisal is to improve the efficiency of an enterprise by attempting to mobilize the best possible efforts from individuals employed in it. Such appraisals achieve our objectives including the salary reviews the development and training of individuals, planning job rotation and assistance promotions.

According to Wendell French, "Performance appraisal and review in the formal, systematic assessment of how well employees are performing their jobs in relations to establish standards and the communication of that assessment to employees.

According to Cascio Wayne, "Performance appraisal is the systematic description of an employee's job relevant strengths and weaknesses.

CHARACTERISTICS OF PERFORMANCE APPRAISAL

The main characteristics of performance appraisal are:

- It is a formal systematic procedure involving usually three steps: setting work standards, assessing employee's actual performance against set standards and provide feedback to the employees to improve deficiencies.
- It is to find out how well the employee is performing the job.
- Employee knows that they are being evaluated.
- The focus of the performance appraisal is measuring and improving the actual performance of the employee and also the future potential of the employee.
- Performance appraisal is not job evaluation.
- It is a future oriented activity as it aims on employee development.

- It is either formal or informal, but formal is more objective as well systematic.

OBJECTIVES OF PERFORMANCE APPRAISAL

The following objectives of performance appraisal are:

1. For Employees: Individual based

- **It is one of the criteria for promotion :** It is one of the yardsticks which can be used as controlling method because the performance reports are considered at the time of promotion especially when the promotion is through seniority basis.

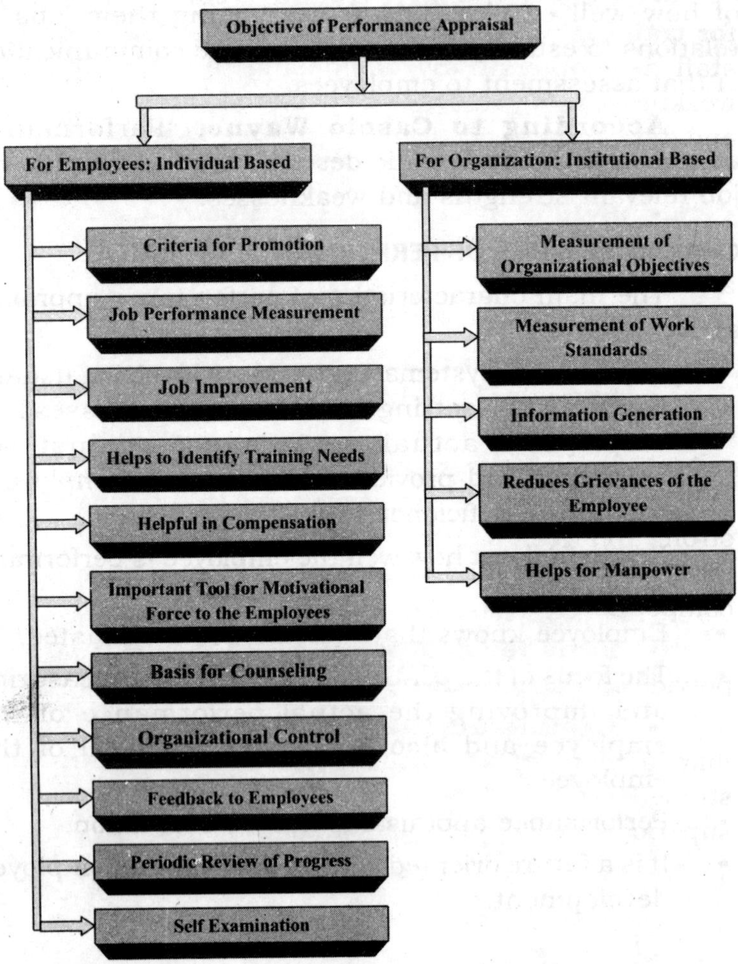

- **Job performance measurement :** The foremost objective of performance appraisal to measure what an employee does or to review the performance of the employees over a given period of time. So she or he will come to know its strengths and weakness and where they stand. And thereby helps to judge the gap between the actual and the desired performance.

- **Job improvement :** When the employees come to know their shortcomings and merits and the management ask them to improve on those points hence it is through performance appraisal they get the opportunity to improve upon weak points.

- **Helps to identify training needs and planning for training programmes :** This is important in case of staff development. By diagnosing the strengths and weaknesses of the individuals helps to identify the training and development needs of the future and accordingly the training programmes can be planned by the employers.

- **Helpful in compensation administration :** This is especially in the private organizations, where the salary and wages are decided according to the employees' performance. In the government can be planned by the employers.

- **Important tool for motivational force to the employees :** At the time of evaluation the administration come to know about employees strengths and weaknesses and at the same time, employee come to know about their strong and weak points. So it becomes motivational force for them to become more efficient and also develop competition attitude among team members.

- **Basis for counseling :** Performance appraisal provides a base for counseling required.

- **Organizational control :** It helps the management in exercising organizational control and strengthens the relationship and communication between superior-subordinates and management-employees.

- **Feedback to employees :** It is through performance appraisal that provides feedback to the employees regarding their past performance.
- **Periodic review of process :** It helps to have periodical review of progress by identifying individual employee's potentials.
- **Self examination :** It affords an opportunity to the employees for self examination and self evaluation.

2. For Organization: Institutional based

- **Measurement of organizational objectives :** Since the efficiency of an organization is based on the achievement of goals and the appraisal will help to measure and know which objectives are fulfilled and which needs attention.
- **Measurement of work standards :** Firstly the work standards are set and the methods are also selected to measure those standards. Later the analysis has been done after measuring actual performance based on work standards.
- **Information generation :** Provide information to assist in the other personal decisions in the organization.
- **Reduces grievances of the employee :** Since for performance appraisal clarity of the expectations and responsibilities of the functions to be performed by the employees if made and that reduces the grievance of the employee.
- **Helps for manpower :** Since the performance appraisal methods are based on job analysis the results of job analysis can be used for planning the number of persons required for a particular job planning and judges the effectiveness of the other human resource functions of the organization such as recruitment, selection, training and development.

ADVANTAGES OF PERFORMANCE APPRAISAL

It is said that performance appraisal is an investment for the company which can be justified by following advantages:

1. Promotion : Performance Appraisal helps the supervisors to chalk out the promotion programmes for efficient employees. In this regards, inefficient workers can be dismissed or demoted in case.

2. Compensation : Performance Appraisal helps in chalking out compensation packages for employees. Merit rating is possible through performance appraisal. Performance Appraisal tries to give worth to a performance. A compensation package which includes bonus, high salary rates, extra benefits, allowances and pre-requisites are dependent on performance appraisal. The criteria should be merit rather than seniority.

3. Employees Development : The systematic procedure of performance appraisal helps the supervisors to frame training policies and programmes. It helps to analyze strengths and weaknesses of employees so that new jobs can be designed for efficient employees. It also helps in framing future development programmes.

4. Selection Validation : Performance Appraisal helps the supervisors to understand the validity and importance of the selection procedure. The supervisors come to know the validity and thereby the strengths and weaknesses of selection procedure. Future changes in selection methods can be made in this regard.

5. Communication : For an organization, effective communication between employees and employers is very important. Through performance appraisal, communication can be sought for in the following ways:

- Through performance appraisal, the employers can understand and accept skills of subordinates.
- The subordinates can also understand and create a trust and confidence in superiors.

- It also helps in maintaining cordial and congenial labour management relationship.
- It develops the spirit of work and boosts the morale of employees.

6. Motivation : Performance appraisal serves as a motivation tool. Through evaluating performance of employees, a person's efficiency can be determined if the targets are achieved. This very well motivates a person for better job and helps him to improve his performance in the future.

TRAINING AND DEVELOPMENT

INTRODUCTION

Training and development play an important role in the effectiveness of organizations and to the experiences of people in work. Training has implications for productivity, health and safety at work and personal development. All organizations employing people need to train and develop their staff. Most organizations are cognizant of this requirement and invest effort and other resources in training and development. Such investment can take the form of employing specialist training and development staff and paying salaries to staff undergoing training and development. Investment in training and development entails obtaining and maintaining space and equipment. It also means that operational personnel, employed in the organisation's main business functions, such as production, maintenance, sales, marketing and management support, must also direct their attention and effort from time to time towards supporting training development and delivery. This means they are required to give less attention to activities that are obviously more productive in terms of the organisation's main business. However, investment in training and development is generally regarded as good management practice to maintain appropriate expertise now and in the future.

MEANING OF TRAINING

Training refers to the process of imparting specific skills. An employee undergoing training is presumed to have had some formal education. No training program is complete without an element of education. Hence we can say that Training is offered to operatives.

MEANING OF DEVELOPMENT

Development means those learning opportunities designed to help employees to grow. Development is not primarily skills oriented. Instead it provides the general knowledge and attitudes, which will be helpful to employers in higher positions. Efforts towards development often depend on personal drive and ambition. Development activities such as those supplied by management development programs are generally voluntary in nature. Development provides knowledge about business environment, management principles and techniques, human relations, specific industry analysis and the like is useful for better management of a company.

CONCEPT OF TRAINING AND DEVELOPMENT

The concept of Training and development can be described as "An educational process which involves the sharpening of skills, concepts, changing of attitude and gaining more knowledge to enhance the performance of employees".

DEFINITION OF TRAINING

According to Dale S. Beach defines training as, "the organized procedure by which people learn knowledge and/or skill for a definite purpose". Training refers to the teaching and learning activities carried on for the primary purpose of helping members of an organization acquire and apply the knowledge, skills, abilities, and attitudes needed by a particular job and organization.

According to Edwin Flippo, "training is the act of increasing the skills of an employee for doing a particular job".

DEFINITION OF TRAINING AND DEVELOPMENT

Training & development is any attempt to improve current or future employee performance by increasing an employee's ability to perform through learning, usually by changing the employee's attitude or increasing his or her skills and knowledge.

Training and development is a subsystem of an organization which emphasize on the improvement of the performance of individuals and groups.

IMPORTANCE OF TRAINING AND DEVELOPMENT

- Optimum utilization of Human resources.
- Development of skills.
- To increase the productivity.
- To provide the zeal of team spirit.
- For improvement of organization culture.
- To improve quality, safety.
- To increase profitability.
- Improve the morale and corporate image.

REASONS TO GO FOR TRAINING AND DEVELOPMENT

- When management thinks that there is a need to improve the performances of employees.
- To set up the benchmark of improvement so far in the performance improvement effort.
- To train about the specific job responsibility.
- To test the new methodology for increasing the productivity.

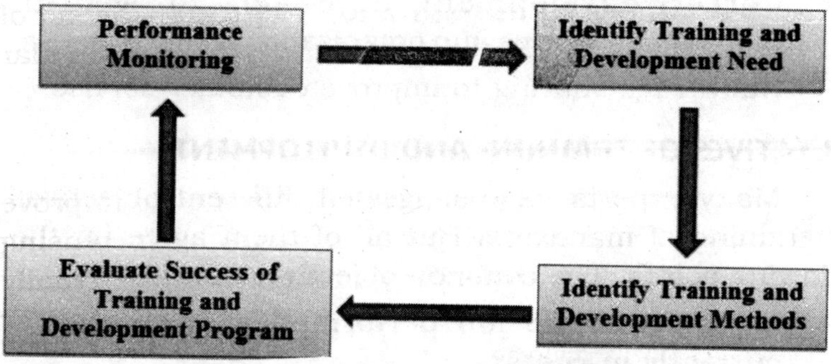

NEED OF TRAINING AND DEVELOPMENT

Individual level

- Diagnosis of present problems and future challenges.
- Improve individual performance or fix up performance deficiency.
- Improve skills or knowledge or any other problem.
- To anticipate future skill-needs and prepare employee to handle more challenging tasks.
- To prepare for possible job transfers.

Group level

- To face any change in organization strategy at group levels.
- When new products and services are launched.
- To avoid scraps and accident rates.

HR ROLE IN TRAINING AND DEVELOPMENT

- Training for tasks leading to successful business operation.
- An in-depth understanding of the business environment.
- An insight regarding training and development options.

- Career development approach to weld-in individuals/groups into organizational effectiveness.
- Knowledge sharing to improve customer service.

OBJECTIVES OF TRAINING AND DEVELOPMENT

Many experts have suggested different objectives for training of managers. But all of them agree on the following points. The common objectives of are:

- To improve the job performance of managers currently in post.
- To provide adequate 'cover' in the event of unexpected short-term changes such as deaths, transfers, resignations or any other unanticipated developments.
- To raise the general level of management thinking and understanding in all branches and at all levels in the organization.
- To provide supply of managerial talent this will fulfill the anticipated needs of the future development of the organization in terms of environmental change and growth.
- To extend the frontiers of knowledge in the understanding of the management function.
- To give the specialists an overall view of the functions of an organization and equip them to coordinate each other's efforts effectively.
- To increase the morale of the members of the management group.
- To improve thought process and analytical ability.
- To broaden the outlook of the executive regarding his role/position and responsibilities.
- To understand the conceptual issues relating to economic, social and technical areas.
- To understand the problems of human relations and improve human relations skills.

- To stimulate creative thinking (Rao, 1992).

DIFFERENCE BETWEEN TRAINING AND DEVELOPMENT

Sr. No	Difference	Training	Development
01	Skill Focus	Training is skills focused	Development is creating learning abilities
02	Formal education	Training is presumed to have a formal education	Development is not education dependent
03	Lack or deficiency	Training needs depend upon lack or deficiency in skills	Development depends on personal drive and ambition
04	Need based	Trainings are generally need based	Development is voluntary
05	Focused on job	Training is a narrower concept focused on job related skills	Development is a broader concept focused on personality development
06	Training	Training may not include development	Development includes training wherever necessary
07	Aim	Training is aimed at improving job related efficiency and performance	Development aims at overall personal effectiveness including job efficiencies

TRADITIONAL AND MODERN APPROACH OF TRAINING AND DEVELOPMENT

Traditional Approach : Most of the organizations before never used to believe in training. They were holding the traditional view that managers are born and not made. There were also some views that training is a very costly affair and not worth. Organizations used to believe more in executive pinching. But now the scenario seems to be changing.

Modern approach : Modern approach of training and development is that Indian Organizations have realized the importance of corporate training. Training is now considered as more of retention tool than a cost. The training system in Indian Industry has been changed to create a smarter workforce and yield the best results.

METHODS OF TRAINING AND DEVELOPMENT

- In-basket training.
- Distance learning & video conferencing.
- Computer-based training.
- Virtual reality.
- E-learning.
- On-the-job training (OJT).
- Job rotation.
- Internships.
- Classroom training.
- Mentoring & coaching.
- Case study.
- Behavior modeling.
- Role playing.
- Apprenticeship training.
- Simulations.
- Business games.

REFERENCES

- Rao, P. Subba. (1992). Essentials of human resource management and industrial relations, Himalaya Publishing House, Delhi, pp. 282-283.

Unit III
LIBRARY ENVIRONMENT

- ***Library Committee** : Introduction, Meaning, Definition, Types, Need, Functions and Power of Library Committee, Characteristics, Responsibilities of the Librarian toward Library Committee.*
- ***Library Organizational Structure** : Introduction, Library Organizational Structure.*
- ***Ranganathan Staff Formula** : Introduction, Development of Staffing Patterns, Status of Staffing Pattern, Ranganathan Staff Formula, Staff Pattern for Public Libraries.*

Library Committee

INTRODUCTION

The library committee consists of a group of persons who are empowered to do certain jobs relating to library and administration. The library committee includes a chairman, a secretary, members or a convener or members. The library committee which has an enormous power to select the library personnel, to acquisition books and journals, which responsible for the fund raising. The committee member though working closely with the librarian but it has some collective powers to run a library smoothly.

MEANING OF LIBRARY COMMITTEE

Library committee is a power which has some important rights and power to controlling all the activities of an institution.

DEFINITION

According to W. H Newman, "A committee consists of a group of people specially designated to perform some administrative work".

According to Krishan Kumar, "A library committee is a body or an organization consisting of persons assigned a particular job".

According to Brian Young, "A library committee is

such a body which is responsible for all the matters pertaining to the efficient library management".

TYPES OF LIBRARY COMMITTEE

A library may have a number of committees depending upon its size and number of activities and operations. The entire library committee can be broadly classified into following six kinds.

1. Self-perpetuating committee : It is created by the particular statue which established the library itself. It is practically independent having sole authority as regards the control and management of the library. It has not report to any other higher body about its activities.

2. Nominated/elected committee : It is a smaller body nominated or elected by a large committee or by authorities for looking after certain bodies under it. It delegates certain functions to such a committee.

3. Executive committee : It is a committee with delegated powers by the authority. This committee is one which has full powers in those matters which are delegated to it and it need not report to its decisions to the library authority.

4. Reporting committee : It has got powers to decide the policies within certain limits and its decisions do not require confirmation of the supreme authority but are simply reported to the authority for its information.

5. Recommending Committee : It has no real power but it can recommend certain proposals for governing the library which are subject to the approval of the library authority.

6. Adhoc committee : It is a special committee for the supervision and control of libraries. This committee is or less independent, this committee is also called statutory committee. It takes decisions expeditiously. It can co-opt men of intellect and foresight. Such a committee may also mean a special committee for performing a special job.

NEED OF LIBRARY COMMITTEE

- The librarian requires the library committee to interpret the needs of the library to the committee.
- In the absence of a library committee, the librarian would find him defenseless and unprotected, so the library committee may serve as a safe guard of a librarian.
- To overcome financial troubles, the library committee is too much necessary.
- Working as an active member of a library committee a librarian can prove himself as an efficient administrators.
- The committee assesses the financial needs of the library in accordance with the national library standards.
- The committee ensures understanding between the readers and the library policies.
- The committees having strong voice can easily convince the authorities and the public.
- Keep the librarian alert.
- Helps the librarian in the smooth functioning of the library.
- Appoint qualified and efficient librarian.

FUNCTIONS AND POWER OF LIBRARY COMMITTEE

Powers and functions of a library committee vary according to its nature. The library committees generally serve the following purposes.

1. Library building : A library committee should ensure that a library building is properly decorated, structured and functional, situated centrally and have necessary arrangement for efficient management.

2. Library furniture and fittings : Library

committee also ensure that adequate, standard and comfortable without any dislocation or wastage of money or space.

3. Library staff : Library committee will fix the needed number of staff, their salary scale, promotions and other regulations related to staff development. They will determine certain principles and formulas that will encourage the intellectual and capable person to enter into the profession.

4. Library finance and book collection : The library committee will raise enough funds for purchasing books and making the collection rich and suitable for the committee to be served. If necessary they will appoint sub-committee for the job.

5. Library rules : Efforts should be made by the library committee to frame a set of library rules that will be flexible to suit the needs of the readers.

6. Library accounts and audit : Proper machinery should be established by the library committee to check the library account. It may appoint an accounts sub-committee for auditing the accounts.

7. Library acts and rules : A library committee should keep library acts and rules up-to-date. The rules and acts which depend on the nature of library must be kept in mind.

8. Standard library service : A library committee should put in its best efforts to secure full coverage and standard library service by opening new branches and by providing more books and staff numbers.

9. Library cooperation : A library committee should find out ways and means of securing cooperation between various branches within a locality and between other authorities especially educational ones.

10. Library policies : It should lay down a policy for the guidance of the librarian for general day-to-day administration of the library.

CHARACTERISTICS OF LIBRARY COMMITTEE

- Use of power.
- Impressive personality.
- Experience and knowledgeable person.
- Impress to library personal.
- Expectation from library personnel.
- Scope of authority.

RESPONSIBILITIES OF THE LIBRARIAN TOWARD LIBRARY COMMITTEE

- Suggestions for policy making
- Apply all the policy and plan created by library committee
- Suggest for selection of library personnel
- Suggest for creating annual budget of library
- According to requirement.
- Help in creating annual report.
- Help in controlling staff activities.

LIBRARY ORGANISATIONAL STRUCTURE

INTRODUCTION

An organizational structure is a way of describing the relationships among groups and individuals in an organization. At the heart of an organizational structure are two things: roles/responsibilities and communications /accountability. Roles and responsibilities refer to what a person or group does, and communications/ accountability involves the relationships that a person or group needs to hold in order to perform their job. It is important to note that even egalitarian or "flat" structures require some kind of relationship in order to perform effectively.

These roles and responsibilities often fall under the three "Ps": "purpose," "people," and "process." A purpose role would describe a group or division through some kind of function. For instance, a "circulation" department is a functional group because people are expected to ensure the effective circulation of materials. A people role focuses on a specific group. "Youth services" would be a good example of a people-oriented role. A process role (sometimes called a "corporate" role — meaning that their job permeates throughout an organizational body) focuses on coordinating among the different function and people roles. Human Resources is probably the most recognizable "process" role.

LIBRARY ORGANIZATIONAL STRUCTURE

The library organizational structure is informed by:

- A commitment to flatter hierarchies and a team-based organisation.
- Balancing workloads through improved structures.
- Facilitating knowledge sharing, communication and empowerment.
- Developing innovative models for communication and client service.
- Balancing professional and non-professional positions to meet requirements and maximize the effectiveness of budget allocation.
- Augmenting human capacity with technological solutions and automation of processes.
- Enhancing flexibility and diversity through full-time, part-time and casual employment.

Teams form the basis of the structure. In order to meet present and future needs, teams may be formed, restructured, merged or disbanded.

LIBRARY - ORGANISATIONAL STRUCTURE, 4 July 2016

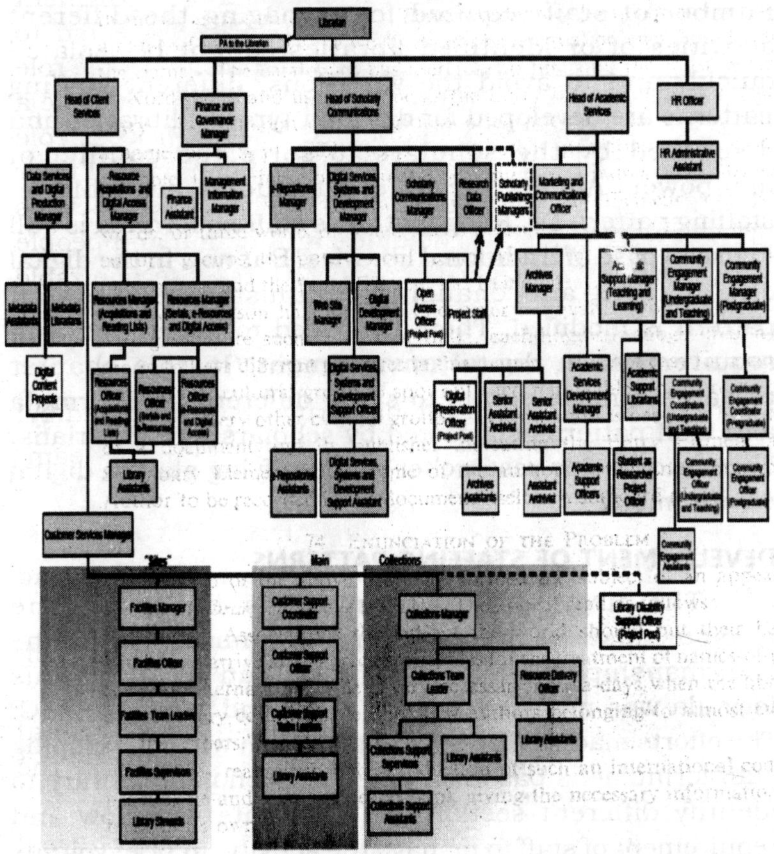

RANGANATHAN'S STAFF FORMULA

INTRODUCTION

Library is an important asset in the society and whereas academic libraries are segment of social institutes and are responsible for capturing and disseminating knowledge to the users. UGC plays an import role in academic sector and support financially to academic libraries for building qualitative collection, to provide different services from the libraries and to acquire literature trained library staff to become qualified staff who can handle efficient tasks in any environment. The number of staff required for managing the different activities of or identified libraries cannot be isolated quickly and to avoid the variations, different staffing patterns are developed for different types of libraries and discussed by the scholars to solve the conflict of manpower. Among the different studies available on staffing pattern Dr. Ranganathan's staffing formula is still in use in case of traditional libraries. But now in the digital environment and changing circumstances the staff pattern is modified. There is a need to review the staff requirement in digital environment. In this chapter researcher made efforts to study different staff formula and staff patterns suggested by scholars and librarians. This study helps researcher in identifying staff in digital environment.

DEVELOPMENT OF STAFFING PATTERNS

The first staffing formula is based on the recommendations made by library committee under the chairmanship of Dr. S R Ranganathan in 1958. This formula was modified later in 1965 and 1979 by UGC. The efforts made by Dr S R Ranganathan while developing staff formulae is based on different sections of library to identify different sections of library its workflow and requirement of staff to manage the activity. In brief volume of documents and providing services to the users is the main base. This formula is suitable for printed media and physical entities added to the library and information centers.

STATUS OF STAFFING PATTERN

The researcher has decided to identify staff pattern for academic environment as this is the major component in higher education society. The academic environment mainly covered college and university libraries due to their nature of work, Colleges are now acting as research centers and getting help from all the academic resources like UGC (IINFONET). On reviewing the literature it is observed that following major staffing patterns in terms of staffing formula are identified by many scholars. A brief analysis of staffing patterns is discussed as under.

RANGANATHAN STAFF FORMULA

Dr. S. R. Ranganathan in his book "Library Administration" 2nd edition has recommended the following staff formula based on intake of libraries

1. Professional staff Pattern : The formula stated by Dr. Ranganathan is :

SB+ SC+ SL+ SM+ SP+ SR+ ST

Where: a) S = Staff

2. Non-professional skilled staff

B/30,000+ S/100

3. Unskilled staff

SB/4+SC/2+SL+SM/4+SP/2+SR/8+A/20,000+D/500+B/60,000+(S/100)/4+V/30,000

Explanation

SB = Number of persons in book section.

SB = A / 6000 = Number of books accessioned in a year/6000.

SC = Number of persons in circulation section.

SC = G / 1500= Number of gate-hours for a year/1500. One gate hour = one counter gate kept open for one hour.

SL = Number of persons as librarian and his deputies = HW/1500= Number of hours library is kept open in day* Number of working days in a year/1500.

SM = Number of persons in maintenance section = A/3000 = Number of volumes accessioned in a year/3000.

SP = Number of persons in a periodicals section = P/500 = Number of periodicals currently taken/500.

SR = Number of persons in reference section =(R/ 50) (W/250) = (Number of readers per day/50) (Number of working days in a year/250).

ST = Number of persons in technical- that is classification and cataloguing-section= A+40D/ 2000=Number of volumes accessioned in a year+ 40* Number of periodicals abstracted and indexed in a year/ 2000.

B = Annual budget allotment in rupees.

S = Number of seats for readers.

A = Number of volumes accessioned in a year.

D = Number of periodicals abstracted and indexed in a year.

V = Number of volumes in the library.

It may be noted that requirement of staff for each section has been calculated on the basis of experience. According to formula, the number of professionals required for a periodical section is based on the assumption that one professional is sufficient for procuring and recording 500 periodicals per year. Similar assumptions form the basis of the formula.

STAFF PATTERN FOR PUBLIC LIBRARIES

S.R. Ranganathan has also recommended the following staff formula for the public library system, which is different than academic libraries but treated mostly important in society development (Krishan Kumar, 1987).

Summary : The staffs required in the library based on Dr Ranganathan formula in different sections are:

1. Book Section : One person for every 6,000 volumes, added in year.

2. Periodical section : One person for every 1,000 periodicals currently taken.

3. Classification and Cataloguing Section : One person for every 2,000 volumes added per year.

4. Maintenance Section : One person for every 2,000 volumes added in a year and one person for every 50,000 volumes in the library for maintaining the total collection.

5. Publicity Section : Minimum one artist.

6. Administrative Section : Minimum one library accountant, one steno-typist and one correspondence clerk are necessary to take care of administration.

7. Reference Section : One person for every 50 readers using the library in a day of the year.

8. Circulation Section : One person for every 1,500 hours for which one wicket-gate of the library has to be kept open in a year.

9. Supervisory Section : One librarian and one deputy librarian.

The professional and non-professional staff that may be required for a public library service has been estimated by the advisory committee for libraries set up by the government of India (Krishan Kumar, 2003) as follows:

1. State Central Library : One state librarian, one deputy librarian, one assistant librarian, twenty-two Non-professionals.

2. District Library : One librarian, one assistant librarian, three professional assistants and nine other non-professional personnel's.

3. City Library : One librarian, one deputy librarian, (except in cities with a population of less than 5 lakhs), one assistant librarian (except in cities with a population of less than 2 lakhs), professional assistants minimum 2, and maximum 18 according to population served.

4. City Branch Library : One librarian, two professional assistants and five non-professional personnel's.

5. Mobile Library : Two professional assistants and three other personnel's.

6. Block Library : One librarian and two other personnel's.

These public libraries staff need is also suggested. But it is very sure that this staff strength is not available in any of the libraries and has to consider the issue.

Unit IV
MOTIVATIONAL PATTERNS

Motivation : *Introduction, Meaning of Motivation,*

- *Traditional and Modern Approach of Motivation,*
- *Definition of Motivation,*
- *Characteristics of Motivation,*
- *Need and Importance of Motivation,*
- *Process of Motivatior,*
- *Sources of Motivation,*
- *Theories of Motivation*
- *Maslow's Theory*
- *ERG THEORY*
- *Herzberg's Two-Factor Theory*
- *McClelland's Theory of Needs*
- *Douglas McGregor Theory of "X" AND Y"*
- *Goal Setting Theory*
- *Reinforcement Theory*
- *Equity Theory*

Motivation Process

MOTIVATION

INTRODUCTION

Motivation is an importance factor which encourages persons to give their best performance and help in achieving the organizational goals. Positive motivation will enable the increased efficiency and negative motivation decreases it among the employees. Motivation is one of the key factors for the personnel management. Motivation is derived from two words i.e. motive (inner state that energies, activates, moves and directs or channel behavioral goals) and action (inducing the motive). Motivation is an amplifying factor for performance.

Performance = Motivation × knowledge + Skill + Ability

MEANING OF MOTIVATION

Motivation is a transitive form of the noun, 'Motive'. Motive is derived from the Latin word, "Move're" meaning 'To Move'. Motivation is the act or process by which the needs and desires of a person move him towards some action.

TRADITIONAL APPROACH OF MOTIVATION

Motivation is not a new concept. It has been practiced from time immemorial albeit, in a different manner. The traditional approach to motivation is called, "Carrot and Stick" approach, where an employee is offered with reward (salary) for his/her performance and punished for non-performance.

MODERN APPROACH OF MOTIVATION

Modern approach to motivation is based on identifying the various needs and wants of an employee and subsequently using them as a means of the driving force behind an employee's action that will in turn have a bearing on the organizations' goals as a whole.

DEFINITION OF MOTIVATION

Motivation is an inspirational process which impels the members of the team to pull their weight effec-tively to give their loyalty to the group, to carry out the tasks properly that they have accepted, and generally to play an effective part in the job that the group has undertaken.

According to Michael Jucious, 'Motivation is the act of stimulating someone or oneself to get a desired course of action, to push the right button to get a desired reaction'.

According to Zedeek and Blood defines, 'Motivation is a predisposition to act in a specific goal-directed way'.

According to Stephen P. Robbins, "Motivation is the processes that accounts for an individual's intensity, direction and persistence of efforts towards attaining a goal".

Motivation is internal and external factors that stimulate desire and energy in people to be continually interested in and committed to a job, role, or subject and to expert persistent effort in attaining a goal.

CHARACTERISTICS OF MOTIVATION

1. Interaction between the individual and the situation : Motivation is not a personal trait but an interaction between the individual and the situation.

2. Goal-directed behaviour : Motivation leads to an action that is goal oriented. Motivation leads to accomplishment of organizational goals and satisfaction of personal needs.

3. Systems oriented : Motivation is influenced by two forces:

- ***Internal forces*** **:** These forces are internal to the individual, i.e., their needs, wants and nature.
- ***External forces*** **:** These forces are external to the individual, who may be organizational related such as management philosophy, organizational structure, and superior-subordinate relationship, and also the forces found in the external environment such as culture, customs, religion and values.

4. Positive or negative : Positive motivation or the carrot approach offers positive incentives such as appreciation, promotion, status and incentives. Negative motivation or stick approach emphasizes penalties, fines and punishments.

5. Dynamic and complex in nature : Human behaviour is highly complex, and it becomes extremely difficult to understand people at work. Motivation is a dynamic and complex process.

NEED AND IMPORTANCE OF MOTIVATION

Motivation offers several importance's to the organization and to the employees:

- Higher efficiency
- Reduce absenteeism.
- Reduces employee turnover.
- Improves a corporate image.
- Good relations.
- Improved morale.

- Reduced wastages and breakages.
- Reduced accidents.
- Facilitates initiative and innovate.

PROCESS OF MOTIVATION

Motivated people are ill constant state of tension. This tension is relieved by drives towards an activity and outcome that is meant to reduce or relieve such tension. The greater the tension, the more activity will, be needed to bring about relief and hence higher the motivation. Thus the basic motivation process can be depicted as follows:

1. Effort : The amount of effort put into the activity identifies the strength of the person's work-related behaviour. Hard work usually reflects high motivation. A student who works very hard to get top grades can be referred to as highly motivate. A professor who is engaged in research and publishes many high quality articles is exerting extensive effort relating to his job.

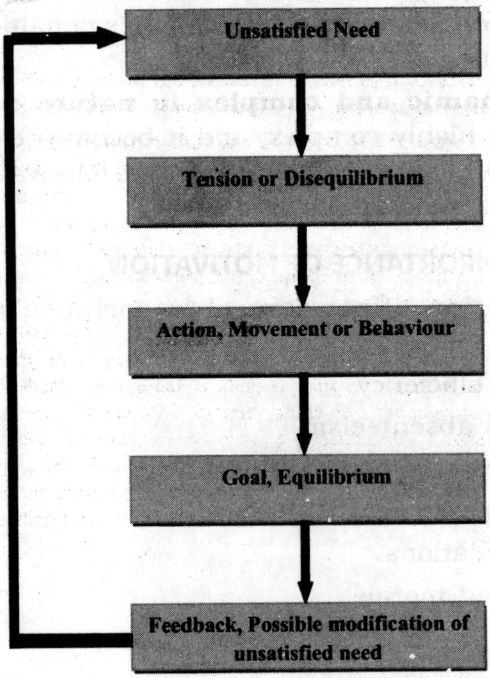

2. Persistence : Motivation is a permanent and an integral part of a human being. Its second characteristic is persistence in the efforts. Motivation is continuously goal directed so that once a goal is achieved, a higher goal is selected and efforts are exercised towards this higher goal. For example, a professor who publishes simply to get a promotion and then stops or reduces research efforts would not be considered as highly motivated. Accordingly, high motivation requires persistent efforts.

3. Direction : Persistent hard work determines the quantity of effort while direction determines the quality of the-anticipated output. All efforts are to be directed towards the organizational goal. This would ensure that the persistent effort is actually resulting into accepted organizational outcomes. For example, a quality control inspector is consistently expected to direct his efforts in discovering defects in the produced items so that the organizational goal of high quality output is met. As an example, let us assume that a professor has established a goal for him to get a promotion and monetary raise in order to improve upon his standard of living. Thus the professor will shape his behavior to achieve that goal. He will thus choose a course of action designed to obtain promotion. This course of action may be five published articles or one published book. He will be highly motivated and will put in persistent efforts in research and publish the desired number of articles or the book. Once the promotion has been obtained the professor will reevaluate his achievement relative' to his initially established objective. If the pay raise is not adequate and there are grounds for further promotion and pay raise, the professor will establish a higher goal and strive towards it. This example fits the basic motivational process as follows:

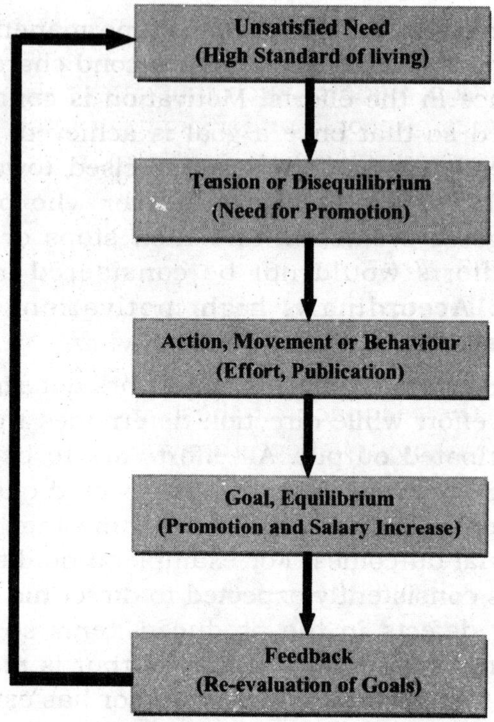

In the above example, if the motivator (publishing) does not serve the required purpose then the professor will look at other alternatives as motivators such as service to the college and community, student guidance and curriculum development, good interactive relations with peers and superiors. Thus the motivation process involves the following steps :

- **Analysis of situation :** The situation that needs motivational inducement must be sized up so as to ascertain the motivational needs. From organizational behaviour point of view it must be recognized that since the needs of different employees differ both in nature as well as intensity, a composite view of the collective needs of the group is established with appropriate recognition of differences in individual needs.

• **Selecting and applying appropriate motivators :** A list of all devices of motivation is drawn and a selection made of such motivators that motivate different types of people under different circumstances. Proper timing and the extent of motivation are also to be considered. The individual goals should be given adequate attention within the framework of group goals and the organizational goals.

• **Follow-up :** It is important to know that the motivators selected are indeed providing the desired motivation. This can be accomplished by getting and evaluating the feedback. If these motivators are not-showing the optimum effect, then alternative motivators should be selected and applied.

SOURCES OF MOTIVATION

Experts in the organizational behaviour field have a divided opinion as to whether workers are motivated by factors in the external environment such as rewards or fear or whether motivation is self generated without the application of external factors. It is quite well understood that under the same set of external factors all workers are not equally motivated. Some of these motivational sources are:

Positive Motivation : Positive motivation involves proper recognition of employee, efforts and appreciation of employee contribution towards the organizational goal achievement. Such motivations improve the standards of performance, lead to good team spirit and pride, a sense of cooperation and a feeling of belonging and happiness. Some of the positive motivators are:

- Praise and credit for work done.
- A sincere interest in the welfare of subordinates.
- Delegation of authority and responsibility to subordinates.
- Participation of subordinates in the decision making process.

Negative or Fear Motivation : This motivation is based upon the use of force, power, fear and threats. The fear of punishment or unfavorable consequences affects the behavioural changes. Some examples of negative motivation include the fear of failing in the examination, and fear of being fired or demoted. Fear of failure in the examination induces motivation in many students to work harder and pass the course. Similarly, fear of being fired keeps the workers in the line with the organizational rules and regulations as well as do a satisfactory job. While the fear of punishment and actual punishment has resulted in controlling individual misbehaviour and has contributed towards positive performance in many situations and is necessary and useful in many other situations such as disciplining a child or handling a riot. It is not recommended or considered as a viable alternative in the current business and industrial environment. This is based upon the trend and changes in the workforce including higher level of employee education and extensive employee unionization. However, punishment or fear of it is still the most common technique of behaviour modification or control in today's life. When a child misbehaves, he is still spanked. If a worker does not be have according to the way the organization wants him to behave, he is fired. If a person does not behave as the society and law wants him to behave, he is punished by arrest and jail. All religions threaten punishment in the life hereafter if a person does not behave according to God's and religious rules.

Extrinsic Motivation : This type of motivation is induced by external factors, which are primarily financial in nature. It is based upon the assumption that the behaviour, which results in positive rewards, tends to be repeated. However, the reward the desired behaviour should be sufficiently powerful and durable so that it improves the probability of occurrence' of desirable behaviour. Money is probably the most important incentive for positive behaviour since money can be used for a number of other resources. These financial incentives and rewards have been a subject of debate whether they really motivate the employees or simply move them to work and perform. These include higher pay, fringe benefits such as retirement plans, stock options, and profit sharing scheme, paid vacation, health and medical insurance, sympathetic supervision and people oriented company policies.

Intrinsic Motivation : Intrinsic motivation stems from feelings of achievement and accomplishment and is concerned with the state of self-actualization in which the satisfaction of accomplishing something worthwhile motivates the employee further so that this motivation is self-generated and is independent of financial rewards. For example, there are many retired doctors who -work free in the hospital because it gives them a sense of accomplishment and satisfaction. Mother Teresa's work in the slums of Calcutta, India, not only motivates the people who work with her but also many others who simply hear about her work and then want to join the team. Similarly, Peace Corps workers work in uncomfortable environments at a minimal pay. Some of the intrinsic motivators are praise, recognition, responsibility, esteem, power, status, challenges and decision-making responsibility.

THEORIES OF MOTIVATION

There are basically two types of theories developed that relate to and define the motivational processes. These are the "content theories" which attempt to determine and specify drives and needs that motivate people to work and "process theories" which attempt to identify the variables that go into motivation and their relationship with each other. These theories are described in greater detail.

The Content Theories of Work Motivation : The

content theories have been developed to explain the nature of motivation in terms of types of need that people experience. They attempt to focus on factors within a person that initiate and direct a certain type of behaviour or check certain other type of behaviour. The basic idea underlying such theories is that people have certain fundamental needs, both physiological and psychological in nature, and that they are motivated to engage in activities that would satisfy these needs. Thus the nature of needs establishes the nature of motivation that results in a specific behaviour aimed at reaching the goal of satisfying such needs. Some of the more important content theories are:

1. Maslow's Theory : Maslow's "needs hierarchy theory" is probably the most widely used theory of motivation in organizations. Abraham Maslow suggested that people have a complex set of exceptionally strong needs and the behaviour of individuals at a particular moment is usually determined by their strongest need. He developed his model of human motivation in 1943, based upon his own clinical experience and formulated his theory of hierarchical needs by asking the same question, what is it that makes people behave the way they do and made a list of answers from which he developed a pattern. His theory is based upon two assumptions. First those human beings have many needs those are different in nature ranging from the biological needs at the lower level, which is the level of survival, to psychological needs at the upper extreme, which is the level of growth. Second that these needs occur in an order of hierarchy so that lower level needs must be satisfied before higher level needs arise or become motivators.

Mahatma Gandhi, the Indian leader, once remarked, "Even God cannot talk to a hungry man except in terms of food. Similarly, there is a quotation from the Holy Guru Granth Sahib, the holy scripture of Sikhs in India when a holy man says to God, "Take your rosary beads away. I cannot worship and meditate on you when I am hungry." This means that if the people's basic needs which are biological in nature are unsatisfied, then their total attention will be focused upon these needs and it will not be possible to communicate with them about other matter. This model of hierarchical needs explains human behaviour in a more dynamic and realistic manner and is primarily based upon people's inner states as a basis for motivation and the environmental conditions do not play any significant role. Maslow postulates five needs basic needs arranged in successive levers. These needs continue to change resulting in change in goes and activities. These five needs are arranged in the form as shown. The first three level needs at the bottom are known as "deficiency" needs, because they must be satisfied in order to ensure the individual's very existence and security and make him fundamentally comfortable. The top two sets of needs are termed "growth" needs because they are concerned with personal growth, development and realization of one's potential.

These needs are explained in detail as follows:

1. Physiological needs : The physiological needs form the foundation of the hierarchy and tend to have the highest strength in terms of motivation. These are primarily the needs arising out of physiological or biological tension and they are there to sustain life itself and include the basic needs for food, water, shelter and sex. Sexual need and desire is not to be confused with love, which is at the third level. Once these basic needs are satisfied to the degree needed for the sufficient and comfortable operation of the body, then the other levels of needs become important and start acting as motivators.

2. Security and Safety needs : Once the physiological needs are gratified, the safety and security need become predominant. These are the needs for self-preservation as against physiological needs, which are for survival. These needs a include those of security, stability freedom from anxiety and a structured and ordered environment. These safety and security needs are really provisions against deprivation of satisfaction of physiological needs in the future. It also involves a sense of protection against threats and danger of losing the job in the future. In a civilized such as ours, a person is usually protected from threats of violence or extremes in climate or fear of material safety, so that the safety and security needs dwell upon economic and job security, life and medical insurance and other protective measures to safeguard the satisfaction of physiological needs in the future which may be unpredictable.

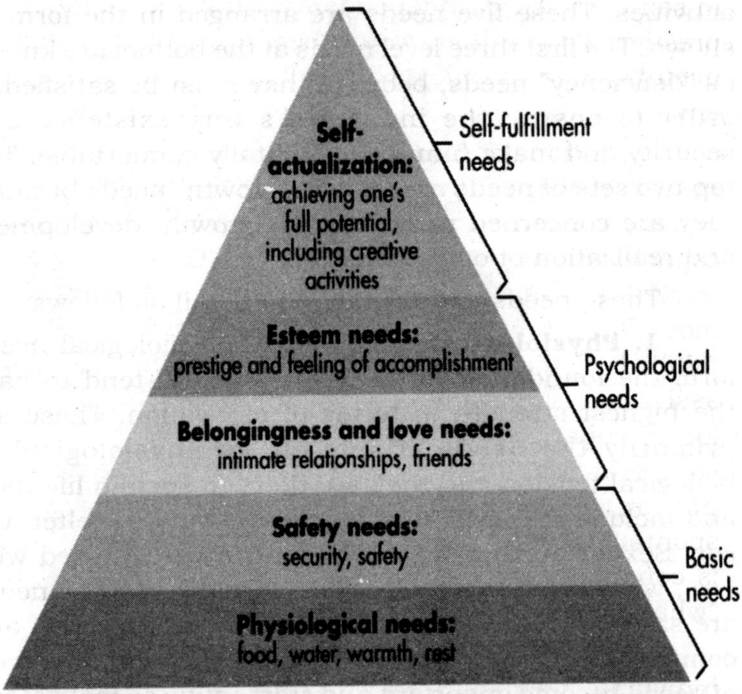

3. Love and Social needs : After the needs of the body and security are satisfied, then a sense of belonging and acceptance becomes prominent m motivating behaviour. These needs include the needs for love, friendship, affection, and social interaction. We look for an environment where we are understood, respected arid wanted. That is one reason for "polarization" where people of similar background arid beliefs tend to group together. "Love thy neighbor" has perhaps a profound meaning.

4. Esteem needs : This need for esteem is to attain recognition from others, which would induce a feeling of self-worth and self-confidence in the Individual. It is an urge for achievement, prestige, status and power. Self-respect is the internal recognition. The respect from others is the external recognition and an appreciation of one's individuality as well as his contribution. This would result in self-confidence, independence, status, reputation and prestige. People then would begin to feel that they are useful and have some positive effect on their surrounding environment.

5. Self-actualization needs : This last need is the need to develop fully and to realize one's capacities and potentialities to the fullest extent possible, whatever these capacities and potentialities maybe. This is the highest level of need in Maslow's hierarchy and is activated as a motivator when all other needs have been reasonably fulfilled. At this level, the person seeks challenging work assignments that allow for creativity and opportunities for personal growth and advancement. This need is for soul searching and is inner oriented. A self-actualized person is creative, independent, content, and spontaneous and has a good perception of reality and he is constantly striving to realize his fun potential. Thus, "what a man 'can' be 'must' be."

Maslow's model is a general model in which an individual needs interact with each other to some degree. Needs are not necessarily linear, nor is the order of needs so rigid. The relative dominance of many needs is variable and is continuously shifting. For example, a self-actualized person may shift his priority to social needs and love needs instead of prestige and status, if suddenly there occurs a vacuum due to loss of a loved one. Similarly, a person may not go to the higher need, even when his lower needs are satisfied. It is also likely that a well-prepared elite person may decide to enter a commune where there is overwhelming emphasis on love and affection rather than climb the corporate ladder.

Maslow's theory made management aware that people are motivated by a wide variety of needs and that management must provide an opportunity for the employees to satisfy these needs through creating a physical and conceptual work environment, so that people will be motivated to do their best to achieve organizational goals. The first level needs in the hierarchy, the physiological needs can be satisfied through such organizational efforts and incentives as adequate wages and salary, acceptable working conditions in order to improve comfort and avoid fatigue, more leisure time and acceptable work environment in terms of lighting, ventilation, rest rooms, working space, heat and noise level. Some bonuses and other fringe benefits will be highly motivational.

The second level needs of safety and security can be satisfied through management's initiative to provide life insurance, medical insurance, job security, cost of living increments, pension plans, freedom to unionize, and employee protection against automation. Law in the form of minimum wages, unemployment benefits, and welfare benefits provides the economic security to some degree. Similarly, unions protect employees against discrimination and indiscriminate firing.

Since first level physiological needs and second level security needs are primarily met by business, industrial, societal and legal environment, management must take steps to satisfy higher level needs and must establish as to which of these needs are the stronger sources of motivation. When the third level needs of love and affiliation become motivators, then people find an opportunity in their work environment for establishing friendly interpersonal relation-ships. The management can satisfy these needs by:

- Providing opportunities for employees to interact society with each other through coffee breaks, lunch facilities and recreational activities such as organized sports programs, company picnics and other social get together.
- Creating team spirit by keeping work groups informal wherever possible with friendly and supportive supervision.
- Conducting periodic meetings with all subordinates to discuss matters pertaining to personal achievements and contributions as well as organizational developments.

The fourth level needs of self-esteem involve a feeling of satisfaction and achievement and recognition for such achievement. The management can take the following steps to satisfy these needs:

- Design more challenging tasks and provide positive feedback on performance of employees.
- Give recognition and encouragement for performance and contribution and delegate additional authority to subordinates.
- Involve subordinates in goal setting and decision-making processes.
- Provide adequate training and executive development programs to help employees successfully accomplish their goals and increase their competency on their jobs.
- Provide some of the symbols for status and respect, such as executive level job title, private secretary, privileged parking, promotion, company car, stock options and write-ups about achievements in the company newspapers.

The fifth and top-level needs of self-actualization long for growth arid creativity and the management can take the following steps to satisfy these needs:

- The employees should be given an opportunity to shape their own jobs.
- Give employees the freedom of expression. This will open the channels of communications further and give the employees an opportunity to get involved. .
- Encourage and develop creativity among employees. Creativity is tied in with freedom of expression and freedom of movement.

Maslow believed that from the point of organizational behaviour the management should strive to create an organizational climate, which motivates employees at all, levels of organizational hierarchy. Research has established that top managers generally are more able to satisfy their higher level needs than lower level managers who have more routine jobs. Blue-collar workers who have very little freedom over job operations may not even experience the higher level needs.

2. ERG THEORY

The ERG need theory, developed by Clayton Alerter is a refinement of Maslow's needs hierarchy. Instead of Maslow's five needs, ERG theory condenses these five needs into three needs. These three needs are those of Existence, Relatedness and-Growth. The E, Rand G is the initials for these needs.

1. Existence needs : These needs are roughly comparable to the physiological and safety needs of Maslow's model and are satisfied primarily by material in centimes. They include all physiological needs of Maslow's model and such safety needs which financial and physical conditions rather than interpersonal relations satisfy. These include the needs for sustenance, shelter and physical and psychological safety from threats to people's existence and well being.

2. Relatedness needs : Relatedness needs roughly correspond to social and esteem needs in Maslow's hierarchy. These needs are satisfied by personal relationships and social interaction with others. It involves open communication and honest exchange-of thoughts and feelings with other organizational members.

3. Growth needs : These are the needs to develop and grow and reach the full potential that a person is capable of reaching. They are similar to Maslow's self-actualization needs. These needs are fulfilled by strong personal involvement in the organizational environment and by accepting new opportunities and challenges.

ERG theory differs from Maslow's theory in proposing that people may be motivated by more than one-kind of need at tile same time. While Maslow proposes that in hierarchy of needs, a person will satisfy the lower level needs before he moves up to the next level of needs and will stay at that, need until it is satisfied, ERG theory suggests that if a person is frustrated in satisfying his needs at a given level, he will move back to lower level needs. For example; assume that a manager's existence needs are fully satisfied and he looks for more challenging tasks to satisfy his self-esteem needs. If his efforts are frustrated in meeting these challenges, he will move back to existence needs and may ask for more material benefits.

3. HERZBERG'S TWO-FACTOR THEORY

Fredrick Herzberg and his associates developed the two-factor theory in the late 1950s and early 1960s. As part of a study of job satisfaction, Herzberg and his colleagues conducted in-depth interviews with over 200 engineers and accountants in the Pittsburgh area. The researchers felt that a person's relation to his work is a basic one and that his attitude towards work would determine his organization related behaviour. The respondents were required to describe in detail the type of environment in which they felt exceptionally good about their jobs and the type of environment in which they felt bad about their jobs. It seems natural to believe that people who are generally satisfied with their job will be more dedicated to their work and perform it well as compared to those people who are dissatisfied with their jobs. If the logic seems justified then it would be useful to isolate those factors and conditions that produce satisfaction with the job and those factors, which produce dissatisfaction. These factors are described in detail as follows:

1. Hygiene factors : Hygiene factors do not motivate people. They simply prevent dissatisfaction and MAINTAIN STATUS QUO. They produce no growth but prevent loss. The absence of these factors leads to job dissatisfaction. The elimination of dissatisfaction does not mean satisfaction and these factors simply maintain a "zero level of motivation." For example: if a person indicated "low pay" as a cause of dissatisfaction, it would not necessarily identify ""high pay" as a cause of satisfaction. Some of the hygiene factors are:

- Wages, salary and other types of employee benefits.
- Company policies and administration rules that govern the working environment.
- Interpersonal relations with peers, supervisors and subordinates Cordial relations with all will prevent frustration and dissatisfaction.
- Working conditions and job security. The job security may be in the form of tenure or a strong union could support it.
- Supervisor's technical competence as well as the quality of his supervision. If the supervisor is knowledgeable about the work and is patient with his subordinates and explains and guides them well, the subordinates would not be dissatisfied in this respect.

All the hygiene factors are designed to avoid damage to efficiency or morale and these are not expected to stimulate positive growth. Hawthorne experiments were highly conclusive in suggesting that improvements in working conditions or increments in financial benefits do not contribute to motivated performance. A new plant or upgraded facilities at a plant seldom motivate workers if the workers do not enjoy their work and these physical facilities are no substitute for employee feelings of recognition and achievement.

2. Motivational factors : These factors are related to the nature of work (job content) and are intrinsic to the job itself. These factors have a positive influence on morale, satisfaction, efficiency and higher productivity. Some of these factors are:

- **The job itself :** To be motivated, people must like and enjoy their jobs. They become highly committed to goal achievement and do not mind working late hours in order to do what is to be done. Their morale is high as evidenced by lack of absenteeism and tardiness.

- **Recognition :** Proper recognition of an employee's contribution by the management is highly morale boosting. It gives the workers a. feeling of worth and self esteem. It is human nature to be happy when appreciated. Thus, such recognition is highly motivational.

- **Achievement :** A goal achievement gives a great feeling of accomplishment. The goal must be challenging, requiring initiative and creativity. An assembly line worker finishing his routine work hardly gets the feeling of achievement. The opportunities must exist for the meaningful achievement; otherwise workers become sensitized to the environment and begin to find faults with it.

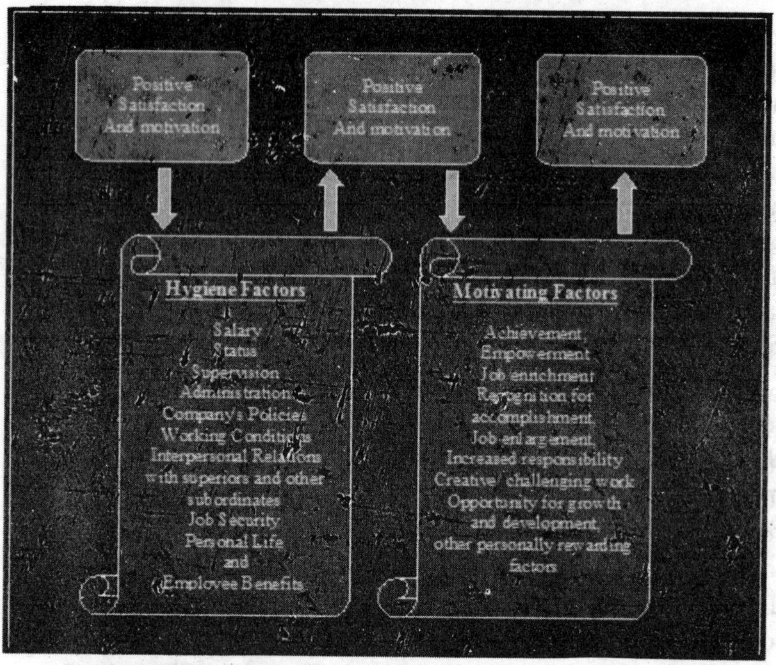

- **Responsibility :** It is an obligation on the part of the employee to carry out the assigned duties satisfactorily. The higher the level of these duties, the more responsible the work would feel and more motivated he would be. It is a good feeling to know that you are considered a person of integrity and be given a higher responsibility. It is a motivational factor that helps growth.

- **Growth and advancement :** These factors are all interrelated and are positively related to motivation. Job promotions, higher responsibility, participation in central decision-making and executive benefits are all signs of growth and advancement and add to dedication and commitment of employees. The Herzberg's two-factor model is tied in with Maslow's basic model in that Maslow is helpful in identifying needs and Herzberg provides us with directions and incentives that tend to satisfy these needs. Also the hygiene factors in Herzberg's model satisfy the first three levels of Maslow's model of physiological needs, security and safety needs and social needs and social needs and the motivational factors satisfy the last two higher level needs of esteem and self actualization.

Some researchers do not agree with Herzberg's model as being conclusive, since the results were based primarily on the responses of white collar workers (accountants and engineers) and do not necessarily reflect the 'blue collar workers' opinion who may consider hygiene factors as motivational factors. Some studies have found that the effect of hygiene factors and motivational factors are totally reversed on some people. They are highly motivated by financial rewards, organized supervision, well-defined work rules, pleasant working environment and positive employee 'interaction and do not give much importance to achievement and self-actualization.

Another criticism about Herzberg's two-factor theory dwells upon the method of research and data collection. The theory was developed on the basis of "critical incident" method. According to this method, the respondents were asked to indicate particular incidents, which they felt, were associated with their satisfaction or dissatisfaction with their jobs. This means that the theory is "method bound" and studies that use other" methods for measuring satisfaction and dissatisfaction fail to support the validity of Herzberg's theory. Furthermore, the theory does not take into consideration individual differences in values and outlook as well as the individual's' age and organizational level. However, this theory has contributed to one management program that has lent itself to the enhancement of motivators. Ii provides valuable guidelines for structuring the jobs in order to include within the job content such factors, which bring about satisfaction.

4. MCCLELLAND'S THEORY OF NEEDS

According to David McClelland, regardless of culture

or gender, people are driven by three motives:

- Achievement.
- Affiliation.
- Influence.

Since McClelland's first experiments, over 1,000 studies relevant to achievement motivation have been conducted. These studies strongly support the theory.

1. Achievement : The need for achievement is characterized by the wish to take responsibility for finding solutions to problems, master complex tasks, set goals, get feedback on level of success.

2. Affiliation : The need for affiliation is characterized by a desire to belong, an enjoyment of teamwork, a concern about interpersonal relationships, and a need to reduce uncertainty.

3. Power : The need for power is characterized by a drive to control and influence others, a need to win arguments; a need to persuade and prevail According to McClelland, the presence of these motives or drives in an individual indicates a predisposition to behave in certain ways. Therefore, from a manager's perspective, recognizing which need is dominant in any particular individual affects the way in which that person can be motivated.

DOUGLAS MCGREGOR THEORY OF "X" AND Y"

Douglas McGregor observed two diametrically opposing viewpoints of managers about their employees, one is negative called "Theory of X" and one is positive called "Theory of Y".

1. Theory of X : Following are the assumptions of managers who believe in the "Theory of X" in regard to their employees.

- Employees dislike work; if possible avoid the same
- Employees must be coerced, controlled or threatened to do the work

Theory X (0%)	Theory Y (100%)
Attitude	
People dislike work, find it boring, and will avoid it if they can.	People need to work and want to take an interest in it. Under right conditions, they can enjoy it.
Direction	
People must be forced or bribed to make the right effort.	People will direct themselves towards a target that they accept.
Responsibility	
People would rather be directed than accept responsibility, which they avoid.	People will seek and accept responsibility, under the right conditions.
Motivation	
People are motivated mainly by money and fears about their job security.	Under the right conditions, people are motivated by the desire to realize their own potential.
Creativity	
Most people have little creativity - except when it comes to getting round rules.	Creativity and ingenuity are widely distributed and grossly underused.

- Employees avoid responsibilities and seek formal direction
- Most employees consider security of job, most important of all other factors in the job and have very little ambition

2. Theory of Y : Following are the assumptions of managers who believe in the "Theory of Y" in regard to their employees.

- Employees love work as play or rest
- Employees are self directed and self controlled and committed to the organizational objectives
- Employees accept and seek responsibilities
- Innovative spirit is not confined to managers alone, some employees also possess it.

Theory of X assumes Maslow's lower level needs dominate in employees. Whereas Theory of Y, assumes Maslow's higher level needs dominate in employees.

5. GOAL SETTING THEORY

Edwin Locke proposed that setting specific goals will improve motivation. Salient features of this theory are the following:

- Specific goal fixes the needs of resources and efforts
- It increases performance
- Difficult goals result higher performance than easy job
- Better feedback of results leads to better to better performance than lack of feedback.
- Participation of employees in goal has mixed result
- Participation of setting goal, however, increases acceptance of goal and involvements.
- Goal setting theory has identified two factors which influences the performance.

These are given below:

1. Goal commitment : Goal commitment: Goal setting theory presupposes that the individual is committed to the goal. This commitment depends on the following:

- Goals are made public
- Individual has an internal locus of control
- Goals are self-set

2. Self-Efficiency : Self Efficiency is the belief or self confidence, that he/she is capable of performing task. Persons with high self-efficiency put up extra-efforts when they face challenges. In the case of low self-efficiency level they will lessen or even abandon when meeting challenges.

The Goal-Setting Theory of Motivation

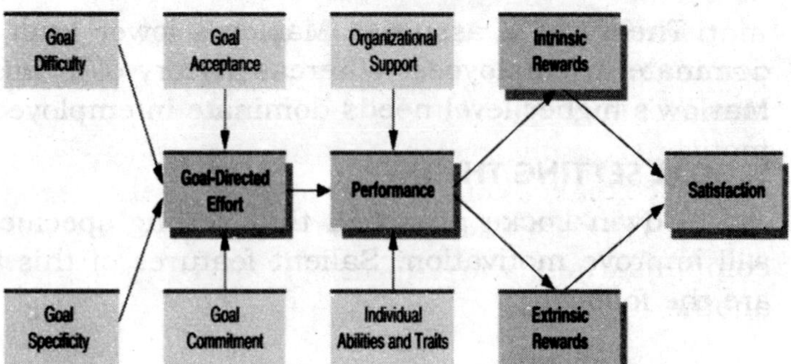

6. REINFORCEMENT THEORY

This theory focuses its attention as to what controls behaviour. In contrast to goal setting theory, this is cognitive approach focus attention on what initiates behaviour. Behaviour, as per cognitive approach is initiated by internal events. Reinforcement theory argues that behaviour is reinforced and controlled by external events. The classical conditioning proposed by Pavlov which we have already studied in our earlier lessons explains this in a better way.

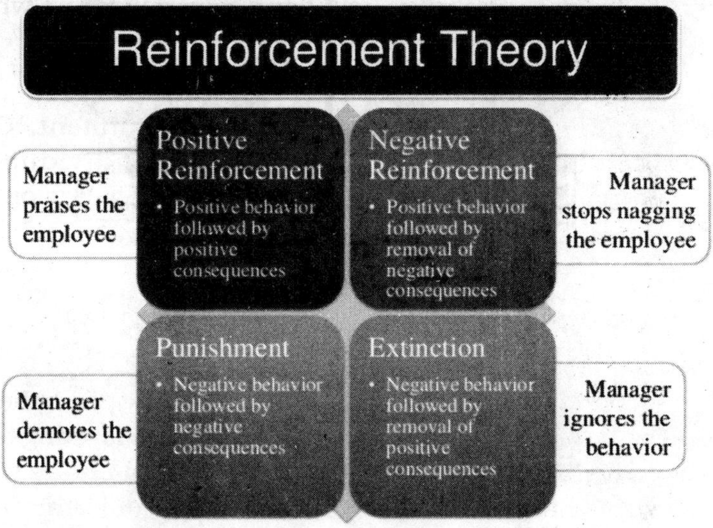

7. EQUITY THEORY

This theory of motivation centres on the principle of balance or equity. According to this theory level of motivation in an individual is related to his or her perception of equity and farness practiced by management. Greater the fairness perceived higher the motivation and vice versa. In this assessment of fairness, employee makes comparison of input in the job (in terms of contribution) with that of outcome (in terms of compensation) and compares the same with that of another colleague of equivalent cadre.

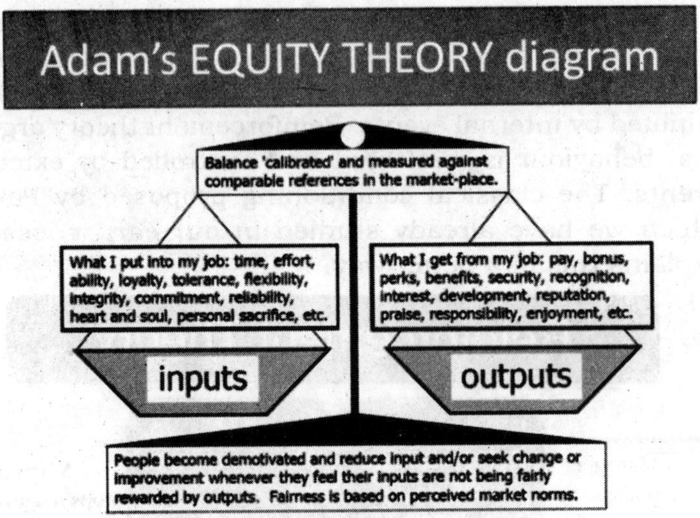
Adam's EQUITY THEORY diagram
Balance 'calibrated' and measured against comparable references in the market-place.
What I put into my job: time, effort, ability, loyalty, tolerance, flexibility, integrity, commitment, reliability, heart and soul, personal sacrifice, etc.
What I get from my job: pay, bonus, perks, benefits, security, recognition, interest, development, reputation, praise, responsibility, enjoyment, etc.
inputs
outputs
People become demotivated and reduce input and/or seek change or improvement whenever they feel their inputs are not being fairly rewarded by outputs. Fairness is based on perceived market norms.

Unit V

LIBRARY PLANNING

- ***Library Planning** : Introduction, Tools and Techniques of Library Planning, Benefits of a Plan, Recipe for a Plan, Phases of a Proposed Library Building, Planning Responsibilities, Some Conceptual Principles of Planning with Modern Libraries.*
- ***Total Quality Management** : Introduction, TQM, Definition, Models of Total Quality Management, Quality Management Tools, Fourteen Steps to TQM, Concept of Library Quality, Benefits of Quality Management in Libraries, Quality Indicators in Libraries, Quality Management in Libraries, Role of Library Managers in TQM, Principles of TQM in Libraries, Elements of TQM, Applications of TQM in Libraries, Benefits of TQM in Libraries, Best Practices for Implementation of TQM in Libraries, Barriers to Implementing to TQM in Libraries*
- ***Quality Standard** : Introduction, What is Quality, ISO-9000 Origin, Aspects of Quality Systems, Structure of ISO-9000, Quality Procedure, Elements of ISO-9000, Benefits from ISO-9000 Certification, The University Library Quality Assurance System, Conclusion.*

Library Planning

LIBRARY PLANNING

INTRODUCTION

Planning is the deliberate, preferred manner of preparing for library service in the future. It is the responsible means of fulfilling future community library needs. A long-range plan, based on knowledge of the community, community expectations, resources of the community, and realistic projections of the future needs of the community will enable the library trustees and administration to perform their responsibilities better by providing efficient and progressive library service.

Every library shall develop, prepare and be guided by a long-range plan. (Planning for Library Excellence Revised [Draft]).

WHAT IS A PLAN?

- A summary of the current status of the library. Look critically at what the library does now. A plan is reality pushed into the future. By assessing the current situation, obvious needs and directions can be identified. Don't be afraid to brag about a good library.
- An assessment of community needs. A library's first responsibility is to address the needs of its community. It is basic planning to know what the

community needs are. The American Library Association has developed a number of tools that can help identify useful statistics and statistical sources for understanding a library's community.

- A statement of the library's mission, goals, and objectives. Once the library's overall role and mission are defined, specific goals with measurable objectives can be set. All decisions should be made in view of the plan.
- An ongoing process. Planning is an ongoing process. No plan is perfect. Unexpected events necessitate changes in any plan, and changing times present new problems and suggest new approaches to meeting library goals. Unless some crisis requires immediate updating of the plan, the plan should be updated on an annual basis.

TOOLS AND TECHNIQUES OF LIBRARY PLANNING

How Is A Plan Developed?

There is no one best way to plan. Planning requires commitment, time, and organization.

1. Preparation for planning requires

- Clarifying planning purposes and methods.
- Defining responsibilities.
- Allocating resources to planning.
- Establishing a planning schedule.

2. Gathering the information for planning requires

- Reviewing community needs for library services including cultural, educational, and informational resources of the community.
- Looking at the demographic and economic data of the community.
- Identifying factors in the library's environment that may affect the provision of services.

3. Analyzing the information allows

- Understanding of the community needs for library service.
- Realizing objectively what the community has and what the community lacks. Defining the library's role in the community.

4. Development of a library's mission, goals, and objectives allows

- Responsiveness to the community's needs, interests, and priorities.
- Prioritizing programs and directing efforts toward tasks leading to the attainment of the stated objectives.
- Evaluation of where your library is in relation to the total plan.

BENEFITS OF A PLAN

- Allows rational justification of your budget with governing authorities.
- Helps you prioritize programs and direct efforts to attaining objectives.
- Motivates the staff and board.
- Encourages coordination and accountability.
- Gives a clear measure for success.
- Assures enough lead time to undertake projects effectively.
- Leads to steady growth by encouraging yearly evaluation.

RECIPE FOR A PLAN

A plan is a flexible document seasoned by specific local needs. Most plans include the following:

- Description of the library's service area and communities

- Summary of data supporting library's needs
- Statement of general goals and specific objectives
- Details of services, programs, personnel, collection, and facilities desired
- Identification of priorities
- Timetable for achieving goals and objectives, both short- and long-range
- Cost projections for implementing the Plan
- Projections of resources
- Assignments and responsibilities for implementing the Plan
- Publicity campaign to accompany changes
- Provision for evaluation and reassessment at specific intervals

PHASES OF A PROPOSED LIBRARY BUILDING

1. Formation of library building committee : It is desirable to form a small building committee to handle the full process of library building. This committee may consist of representative from all concerned groups as well as the architect and the librarian. A building committee should be appointed to assist in the preparation of a concept programme evaluation of building plans. The building committee should consist of the following:

- The architect.
- The librarian.
- The library consultant.
- Interior designer.
- Head of the institution.
- Others.

Responsibility of Library Building committee: The responsibilities of library building committee are:

- The building committee should be charged with the

responsibility for ascertaining the library's needs and for accumulating necessary data.

- The committee should consult as widely as necessary to determine the needs of the library.
- The committee should acquaint itself with the experience of other libraries with respect to new buildings.
- It should visit, if possible, some newer libraries and examine library building plans.
- With the assistance of the librarian and library consultant, the committee should make detailed estimates of the requirements of the different library units.

2. Arranging the library building programme : After building committee has completed it's planning it set down in writing, for the guidance of architect, a detailed, explicit statement of the requirements of the library. This statement may be prepared by the librarian by the library consultant, or by the architect in consultation with librarian or by the building committee itself. Space requirements should be given in detail. These requirements may be stated under such headings as: Space for books, space of readers (Seating), space for staff, and space required for other purposes.

3. Space estimates : In early stages of planning it is helpful to make some rough estimates of space requirements in terms of floor area. These estimates can be used in calculating probable cost of construction and they can be kept in mind when building sites are being considered. There is no standard measure that can be followed everywhere. A probable estimate for public library and for university are given below:

In Public Library

- For Magazine and periodical reader: 12 foot of superficial space each.

- Borrower estimated to be present one time: 20 square foot
- Normal Books: 10 volumes per square foot. But in reference section 7-8 volumes per square foot.

In University Library

- For library materials: 1 square foot per 15 volumes.
- Undergraduate students: 25 square foot per student.
- Graduate students: 35 square foot per student.
- Faculty Member: 75 square foot per member.
- Staff, counting and anticipated size: 100 square foot per person there are space requirements for stairways, corridors, ventilating of air conditioning and other accommodations.

4. The preliminary plans : The preliminary plan represents the most important phase of the whole planning process. The architect may produce a rough drawing of the main floor. The librarian has an important role in this preliminary plan. He should examine critically the architect's first drawing to determine whether adequate provision is being made for each library functions and whether the building as a whole will be sufficiently flexible and expandable for future use. After establishing the arrangement between the architect and librarian, the architect may draw the detail plan. If the cost estimates are satisfactory and no important problems remain, the preliminary plan will be approved and the architect will be authorized to prepare large plan and specifications.

5. Final plans and specifications : Final plans will consist of floor plans, elevations and sections and details of the structure. These will provide graphic illustrations of the building from several physical view points. The general constructions plans will be supplemented by separate set of drawings illustrating the design of the heating, ventilating and air-conditioning systems. There will be additional drawings illustrating the detailed design and location of many general and special features of the building such as stacks furniture etc. This plan will be supported written specifications describing the type and quality of materials to be used and any other information necessary for the builder. Then it can be placed for final approval of the committee.

6. Selecting the site : Where to locate the new buildings is an important question.

According to **K. Metcalf**, five major factors should be considered in selecting a sit.

Those are:

- Is its size adequate?
- What is its relation to neighboring buildings and to the whole population and traffic flow of the institution?
- What orientation is possible for a library building erected on it?
- Are there advantages or disadvantages in the slope of the land?
- What complications will arise from the nature of the ground beneath the buildings?

Simply, the site should be large enough to accommodate the present building and pursuit future expansion. The site should have an excellent surroundings and quiet environment. The library buildings should be situated centrally with pleasant surroundings and convenient accessibility where no contamination of air, sound etc. will occur.

PLANNING RESPONSIBILITIES

Planning for Library Excellence, Revised (Draft) should be consulted for building-related state standards and guidelines. Trustees, staff members, consultants, architects, interior designers, city councils, county boards, jurisdictional staffs, regional planning departments, and community members all fit into the picture.

Trustees

- Determine that a new building is needed.
- Provide leadership in the campaign to inform the community and secure necessary support for the project.
- Appoint a building committee and assign tasks.
- Select and hire library building consultant.
- Select and hire an architect.
- Obtain financing for the project.
- Select and purchase the site.
- Approve the written building program.
- Approve preliminary and final architectural plans
- Solicit and approve bid documents
- Approve all contracts and any change orders to the contract

Library Staff

The library director and staff actively participate in planning for construction projects by compiling information, surveys, and statistics; by helping to prepare a written building program; by preparing building applications and reports; and by maintaining project records. The library director must be a member of the building team for accomplishment of a functional plan to support the library program.

Library Building Consultant

The consultant is usually an experienced librarian who has participated in several building projects. The cost of a building consultant can usually be saved many times over in reductions in construction and operating costs. Working with board and staff the building consultant can provide any or all of the following services:

- Survey the library's space needs
- Write the library building program
- Project a preliminary project budget
- Provide site analysis and recommendations
- Provide advice on funding options
- Provide assistance in selection of the architect
- Review all plans prepared by the architect and provide a written evaluation
- Review needs, specifications, and layout for shelving, furniture, and equipment
- Provide a final inspection of the facility

The Library Building Consultant of the Library Development and Networking Division of the Library of Virginia can provide building consultation advice and guidance.

We're set to go. What's next?

The board, with its planning completed, money in hand, and architecture in the final stages of plans, should follow this sequence:

- Review every nuance of the building plan. Decide what features can be optional (bid alternates) so that separate bids can be taken on these items.
- Review estimated costs so that the construction bids do not surprise.
- Follow all local ordinances and structures. Zoning and building codes should be checked as plans are made, but enlist the help of appropriate officials in the plan review and in recommending contractors to be asked to bid.
- Follow correct bidding procedures, legal and ethical. Allow time for bidders to estimate closely. Invite enough bidders so that there is a range.

- Analyze bids ruthlessly. Be sure you are getting what was specified with no unsuitable substitutes. Accept the bid that most closely meets specifications as well as offering good value.
- All bids too costly? You can call for new bids to an amended set of specifications. You can also rule out the optional features (bid alternatives) that did prove to be too much.
- Create a team of board, director, architect, and contractor to follow progress and to make regular reports.
- Expect some changes. Discoveries will be made about unexpected problems and opportunities. The contractor may suggest, for example, that a new tile may be less expensive and serve just as well as that specified. If so, that's a credit you can apply to something that will cost more (such as discovering poor soil on the site).
- Expect performance. This building is going to be a fixture in the community for a long time and should be properly and expertly built. Some boards find that the contractor has taken the job as a fill-in. doesn't accept excuses!
- Watch the expenditure of funds in a professional manager. Payments should be made upon proper evidence, but promptly. If you need financial advice, seek it from a good mortgage banker or experienced purchaser of construction.
- Meet frequently during the building process. Meetings keep you in touch with progress, permit decisions on changes, and provide the material for ongoing public relations in the community.
- Plan for orderly occupation of the building, when it's ready, with festivities and community involvement. Allow plenty of time for moving in, completing the landscaping and other amenities,

and then showing off the newest and best community asset.

SOME CONCEPTUAL PRINCIPLES OF PLANNING WITH MODERN LIBRARIES

The traditional library doesn't meet the changing needs on information provision of today's information society. Library buildings, which are planned on old norms and standards, do not satisfy today's situation. Summarizing the results of above-mentioned research, we can formulate some principles of modern library's activity and its architectural solutions.

1. The modern public library has to be multifunctional : The modern public library has to be multifunctional and to provide not only informational or other typical library services but cultural, communicational and other extra services as well. Such library will comprise two functional parts: (1) Provision of library's traditional informational services and (2) Cultural and social services. These non-traditional services (cultural, educational, commercial, sports, recreational, entertainment etc.) will make the library more attractive and can lead to an increase of the number of users of the traditional library services.

For this new cultural and social functional part adequate premises have to be planned. This will give the library a new image of social importance. The modern public library will become a social centre of culture, a home for society. It will be a multifunctional and vital centre, organising and joining society. A library with such social and cultural activity will be more attractive for investments. The library will become a library information centre, club, and Internet café etc. Oriented to the various needs of society such a library will satisfy needs of different social groups and ages. It will become a synthesis of various cultural activities. All these different kinds of activity will stimulate other kinds of cultural activities and all kinds of culture in general. So, the public library has to be perceived as an information institution and as an amateur art centre and organizer of recreation and communication as well.

2. The modern public library has to be comfortable : Comfortableness of service is one of the most important indicators of modern library activity's value. This indicator includes: easy access to the library building, rational planning of the building and impressive architecture. There should be created a good working environment in the library: arranged individual carrels for intensive working and studying users, and well illuminated working places with dividing screens separating each place. Comfortableness also includes: providing the library with soft furnishing, plants, aquariums, soft carpet, large windows, balconies, premises for communication of people with different interests, and provisions with sound and video equipment. There is one more important demand for comfortableness. This is the accessibility of the collection. The collection has to be located according to library's collection profile, library's strategy and expectable users. The whole collection, arranged in subject groups, has to be located in different areas of open stacks.

3. The modern library has to exist in harmony with its natural and urban environment : The library has to become an organic part of the natural and urban environment.

4. The modern library as an open, democratic and intellectual communication institution : All architectural solutions of the modern library have to express the image of the library as an open, democratic and intellectual communication institution. This image can be created by planning buildings of "virtual" architecture what can be characterized by "dematerialized" forms of clear, laconic, simple and visible bulks. In the process of making constructional resolutions and choosing the building materials one has to orient on comfortableness of the internal and external environment of the library. There has to be a balanced thermal, illumination and noise regime. The building of a public library has to be not higher than four over ground floors. The higher a building, the more expensive will its maintenance be, more staff will be needed and more sophisticated technology and security systems.

5. Planning of the building has to be flexible and simple : The planning of the building has to be flexible and simple in the general plan. There have to be possibilities of extension or transformation. That's why is advisable to use as much as possible movable columns, equally located ventilation, heating and aeration systems. The construction of light screens should also be easily movable from one to another to create a large space.

6. An internal garden in the middle of a building : It is advisable to design an internal garden in the middle of a building. This solution together with vertical and horizontal cabling allows an architect to create an optimal and aesthetic interior. Through the internal garden it is possible to achieve an architectural wholeness of the building and the interior.

7. Locate the storages on the underground floors : It is advisable to locate the storage-spaces on the underground floors and premises that need daylight on the over ground floors. The underground storage-spaces can be characterized by the following advantages: the possibility of rational usage of the collection, to locate it operatively, to organize more credible security of the collection, and make it much easier to maintain a proper temperature and humidity regime. The underground storage-spaces make it possible to design a compact building, and better its constructional, economic and exploitative indicators.

TOTAL QUALITY MANAGEMENT

INTRODUCTION

An organization planning the implementation of Total Quality Management (TQM) is about to embark on the challenge and opportunity of a lifetime. This adventure must surely change the organization. Total Quality Management can be the answer to both the customer's plea for improved products and services and the organization's quality and productivity problems.

TQM is a "system of continuous improvement employing participative Management and centered on the needs of customers". Key components of TQM are employee involvement and training. Problem solving teams, statistical methods, long term goals, thinking and recognition that the system, not people produces inefficiencies. Libraries can benefit from TQM in three ways: breaking down interdepartmental barriers; redefining the beneficiaries and library services as internal customers (staffs) and external customers (patrons); and reaching a state of continuous improvement.

A library should always focus on providing the best services possible, and be willing to charge to service its customers.

TOTAL QUALITY MANAGEMENT

Total quality management is an approach that an organization takes for improving its performance on systematic and continuous basis. This is achieved by involving all employees throughout the organization in satisfying all requirements of every customer, whoever the customer may be either external or internal. Quality Management is the basis for library management in general. Such principles of TQM as meeting the Customer needs, exact assessment, continuous improvement, team work and enthusiasm of the leaders are typically for library services.

Total : Everyone in the organization is involved in creating and maintaining the quality of the services and the products offered.

Quality : The organization through individual and collections focuses on meeting customer needs, recognizing that customer perception identities quality.

Management : In managing the system, the emphasis les on continuously improving his system in order to achieve the best results.

DEFINITION

TQM is a management philosophy embracing all activities through which the needs of the customer and the community, and the objectives of the organization, are satisfied in the most efficient and the cost-effective way by maximizing the potential of all employees in a continuing drive for improvement.

TQM is a management approach for an organization, centered on quality, based on the participation of all its members and aiming at long-term success through customer satisfaction, and benefits to all members of the organization and to society.

Total Quality management is defined as a continuous effort by the management as well as employees of a particular organization to ensure long term customer loyalty and customer satisfaction. Remember, one happy and satisfied customer brings ten new customers along with him whereas one disappointed individual will spread bad word of mouth and spoil several of your existing as well as potential customers.

MODELS OF TOTAL QUALITY MANAGEMENT

Total Quality Management is a combined effort of both top level management as well as employees of an organization to formulate effective strategies and policies to deliver high quality products which not only meet but also exceed customer satisfaction.

Total Quality management enables employees to focus on quality than quantity and strive hard to excel in whatever they do. According to total quality management, customer feedbacks and expectations are most essential when it comes to formulating and implementing new strategies to deliver superior products than competitors and eventually yield higher revenues and profits for the organization.

Credits for the process of total quality management go to many philosophers and their teachings. Drucker, Juran, Deming, Ishikawa, Crosby, Feigenbaum and many other individuals who have in due course of time studied organizational management have contributed effectively to the process of total quality management.

There are many models of total quality management and it is really not necessary that every organization should select and implement the same model.

Following are the various models of total quality management:

- Deming Appiication Prize
- Malcolm Baldrige Criteria for Performance Excellence
- European Foundation for Quality Management
- ISO quality management standards

Customers and their feedbacks are the foundation of every Total Quality Management model. In simpler words, Total Quality Management begins with understanding customers, their needs and what they expect from the organization. Design foolproof processes and systems to collect customer data, information to further study, analyze and act accordingly. Such activities not only help you understand your target customers but also predict customer behaviour.

As a business marketer, you need to know the age group of your target customers, their preferences and needs. Employees need to know how their products or services can fulfill customer needs and demands. Total Quality Management model requires meticulous planning and research. Every total quality management model integrates customer feedbacks with relevant information and plans accordingly to design effective strategies to achieve high quality products. Strategies formulated to yield better quality products need to be evaluated and reviewed from time to time. Remember, customers are satisfied only when products meet their expectations, fulfill their needs and are value for money. Their overall experience with the organization needs to be pleasant for them to be happy and return to the organization even the next time.

Continuous improvements, changes and modifications in the existing processes according to customer expectations are necessary to yield higher profits. Processes can't be same always. If a customer complaints about a particular product of yours, find out the root cause of problem. Understand and implement necessary total quality management models to rectify the problem, remove the defect for a high quality product.

The successful implementation of Total quality Management model needs extensive planning and most importantly participation of every single member who is benefitted out of the organization (Management, suppliers, clients and even customers). Without the participation of each and every employee, total quality management model would be a complete failure. Total Quality Management model begins with research and collecting information about end-users followed by planning and full participation of employees for successful implementation. Top level Management needs to make other team members aware of the benefits of total quality management process, importance of quality to survive in the long run and how they can implement various TQM models by prioritizing their customers and their feedbacks.

QUALITY MANAGEMENT TOOLS

Quality Management tools help organization collect and analyze data for employees to easily understand and interpret information. Quality Management models require extensive planning and collecting relevant information about end-users. Customer feedbacks and expectations need to be carefully monitored and evaluated to deliver superior quality products. Quality Management tools help employees identify the common problems which are occurring repeatedly and also their root causes. Quality Management tools play a crucial role in improving the quality of products and services. With the help of Quality Management tools employees can easily collect the data as well as organize the collected data which would further help in analyzing the same and eventually come to concrete solutions for better quality products. Quality Management tools make the data easy to understand and enable employees to identify processes to rectify defects and find solutions to specific problems.

Following are the quality management tools:

- **Check List :** Check lists are useful in collecting data and information easily .Check list also helps employees to identify problems which prevent an organization to deliver quality products which would meet and exceed customer expectations. Check lists are nothing but a long list of identified problems which need to be addressed. Once you find a solution to a particular problem, tick it immediately. Employees refer to check list to understand whether the changes incorporated in the system have brought permanent improvement in the organization or not?
- **Pareto Chart :** The credit for Pareto Chart goes to Italian Economist Wilfredo Pareto. Pareto Chart helps employees to identify the problems, prioritize them and

also determine their frequency in the system. Pareto Chart often represented by both bars and a line graph identifies the most common causes of problems and the most frequently occurring defects. Pareto Chart records the reasons which lead to maximum customer complaints and eventually enables employees to formulate relevant strategies to rectify the most common defects.

- **The Cause and Effect Diagram :** Also referred to as "Fishbone Chart" (because of its shape which resembles the side view of a fish skeleton) and Ishikawa diagrams after its creator Kaoru Ishikawa, Cause and Effect Diagram records causes of a particular and specific problem .The cause and effect diagram plays a crucial role in identifying the root cause of a particular problem and also potential factors which give rise to a common problem at the workplace.

- **Histogram :** Histogram, introduced by Karl Pearson is nothing but a graphical representation showing intensity of a particular problem. Histogram helps identify the cause of problems in the system by the shape as well as width of the distribution.

- **Scatter Diagram :** Scatter Diagram is a quality management tool which helps to analyze relationship between two variables. In a scatter chart, data is represented as points, where each point denotes a value on the horizontal axis and vertical axis. Scatter Diagram shows many points which show a relation between two variables.

- **Graphs :** Graphs are the simplest and most commonly used quality management tools. Graphs help to identify whether processes and systems are as per the expected level or not and if not also record the level of deviation from the standard specifications.

FOURTEEN STEPS TO TOTAL QUALITY MANAGEMENT

Based on the work of Japanese managers, Demirs outlined 14 steps that managers in any types of organization can take to implement a total quality management programme.

1. Create constancy of purpose for improvement of product and service. Constancy of purpose requires innovation, investment in research and education. Continuous improvement of product and service, maintenance of equipment, furniture and fixtures and new aids to production.
2. Adopt the new philosophy management must undergo a transformation and begin to believe in quality products and services.
3. Cease dependence on mass inspection. Inspect product and services only enough to be able to identify ways to improve the process.
4. End the practice off awarding business o price tag alone. The lowest priced goods are not always the highest quality.
5. Improve constancy and forever the system of product and service. Improvement is not a onetime effort; management is responsible for leading the organization into the practice of continual improvement in quality and productivity.
6. Institute training and retraining. Workers need to know how to do their jobs correctly even they need to learn new skills.
7. Institute leadership: Leadership is the job of management. Managers have the responsibility to discover the barriers that prevent staff from taking pride in what they do. The staff will know what those barriers are.
8. Drive out fear people often bear reprisal if they "make waves" at work. Managers need to create an environment where works can express concerns with confidence.
9. Break down barriers between staff areas. Managers

should promote teamwork by helping staff in different areas/departments work together. Fostering interrelationship among departments encourages higher quality decision-making

10. Eliminate slogans, exhortations and targets for the workforce. Using slogans alone, without an investigation into the process of the workplace can be offensive to workers because they imply that a better job could be done. Managers need to learn real ways of motivating people in their organization.
11. Eliminate numerical quotas. Quotas impede quality more than another working condition they leave noncoms for improvement. Workers need the flexibility to give customers in level of service they need.
12. Remove barriers to pride of workmanship; give workers respect and feed back about how they are doing their jobs.
13. Institute a vigorous programme of education and retaining. With continuous improvement, job descriptions will change. As a result employees need to be educated and retained so they will successful at new job responsibilities.
14. Take action to accomplish the transformation. Management must work as a team to carry out these above 13 steps.

CONCEPT OF LIBRARY QUALITY

In an ideal world all organizations would have continuous quality improvement programs. They would strive to improve the quality of their products, services, marketing, selling, customer support, employee relations and other functions. Libraries, like many other nonprofit, service and educational organizations, have tended to define quality in terms of richness of resources. Total number of volumes owned, number of bestselling books per site, size of professional staff, and similar measures have been taken as indicators of quality. The quality of library services cannot be achieved without progressing though a series of few basic steps that are common to almost all the systems of evaluation. Under continuous improvement, quality is defined as that which meets or exceeds customer expectations. The implications of this are profound. First, libraries must know what their customers expect and how they measure such expectations. A second implication rests on the first-which libraries have an obligation to ensure that their customers are informed/ educated about what kinds of expectations they could reasonably hold. If traditional measures of quality are no longer valid, decisions must be reached about what new measures are appropriate and how they will be obtained. The literature shows a number of research and articles in library and information science that reflect an interest in most of these dimensions. It has also explored the value that library customers place on services.

We can improve the quality of library service by taking into consideration the following:

- Guidance.
- Waiting time.
- E-Services.
- Library staff (available, courteous, approachable and friendly) and material in their correct place.
- All the library equipments should be kept in good working order.
- Material arriving within a set time.
- The building and the library environment.
- Library furniture and facilities (e.g. drinking fountain).
- Material for course needs.

Tann (1993) suggests that "quality or fitness for purpose" of libraries should include

- Knowing the customer's need.
- Designing a service to meet them on or off the premise.
- Faultless delivery of services.
- Suitable facilities-car parking, café, crèche.
- Good accommodation-seating, lighting, heating, toilets.
- Good housekeeping
- Reliable equipment-computers, videos.
- Efficient administration- welcome, queries answered efficiently and effectively;
- Helpful, courteous staff.
- Monitoring and evaluation including customer expectation, complaints, recommendations for improvement.
- Feedback loops to build in improvement procedures and or checking that improvements are put in place.

Hernon and Alman (1996) indicate that for libraries, quality applies to three general areas, each of which consists of assorted variables:

- Resources: information content.
- Organization: service environment and resource delivery.
- Service delivered by staff.

The literature indicated that quality involves every aspect of library-organization, resources and services, even behind-the-scenes activities.

BENEFITS OF QUALITY MANAGEMENT IN LIBRARIES

If we carefully implement, quality management principles in an academic library it yield the following positive benefits, such as:

- Incremental changes lead to continuous improvement-quick solutions may yield only partial results.
- Forces library managers to develop leadership skills instead of relying on power within position to obtain results.
- Increases staff participation in decision making, thus increasing the feeling of "ownership" of decisions and directions once charted, promotes teamwork.
- Improves the level of training given to staff, thus increasing skills.
- Helps break down barriers between library departments and improve communication within the organization.
- Provides a method of improving services to users in a period of limited resources.
- Improves library management control.
- Improve awareness of quality services.
- Enhance accountability of parent institution.
- Enhance the continuing quality improvement.
- Reduce operating cost.
- Reduce rework.
- Improve library staff moral and attitudes.
- Improve management of library personnel.
- Improve management of library.
- Improve library services.
- Increase library customer satisfaction, focuses on customers.
- Improve documentation.
- Create better understanding among library staff and library customers.

- Provides real solutions rather than temporary solutions.
- Provides uniform tools for evaluation.
- Streamlines processes

QUALITY INDICATORS IN LIBRARIES

Quality is often an indefinable concept. It is difficult (but not impossible) to define and measure, especially when the service is intangible and abstract. The quality of an organization can be measured in many ways: financial results, good employer, zero defects in goods produced, customer satisfaction, successful marketing or innovation. **(Clair, 1997).**

According to Van House, Weil and McClure a set of common criteria to measure academic and research library performance are divided into four groups as follow:

General User Satisfaction

- A user self-reports of success during the library visit on each of several library activities.
- Ease of use of the library.
- Overall satisfaction with today's library visit.
- Create service brochures and information kits.
- Develop Improve the physical layout of the library.
- User and staff training materials.

Materials Available and Use

- Number of items changed out for use, usually (though not always), outside the library, includes initial charges and renewals.
- General collection and reserves.
- Number of items used in the library but not charged out.
- Total number of uses of library materials.
- The sum of circulation and in library material use.

- Proportion of users searches for library materials that are successful at the time of user's visit.
- Time users must wait for requested materials.
- Proportion of users searches for library materials that are successful at the time of user's visit.
- Time users must wait for requested materials number of user's visits to library.

Facilities and Library Use

- Number of library uses for which users does not come to the library, such as use of document delivery services, access to library catalogs or other online databases maintained by the library from terminals outside the library, or telephone, e mail, or fax requests for materials or services. Offer electronic document delivery.
- Total uses of library, in-person and remote.
- Sum of attendance and remote uses.
- Proportion of time, on average, that a facility is busy.
- Facilities include user seating and workstations and user equipment such as photocopy machines.
- Average number of users at a service point.
- Service points are staffed public service sites: e.g. circulation, reference and information desks.
- Average number of people in library at any one time.
- Create interdepartmental library advisory.

Groups Information Services

- Number of reference transactions. A reference transaction is an information contact that involves the knowledge, use, recommendations, interpretations or instruction of one or more information sources by a member of the library staff.
- Users evaluation of the outcome of reference transactions, the service experience, and overall

satisfaction with the reference service.

- Users report of satisfaction with performance of the search intermediary and the search product and overall satisfaction with the online search.

QUALITY MANAGEMENT IN LIBRARIES

TQM is now practiced in business as well as in government, the military, education, and in non-profit organizations including libraries. Libraries can benefit from TQM in three ways:

- Breaking down interdepartmental barriers.
- Redefining the beneficiaries of library services as internal customers (staff) and external customers (patrons).
- Reaching a state of continuous improvement (**Jurow & Barnard, 1993**).

The practice of Quality Management in Library & Information Science sector existed since the evolution of the subject itself, but the terminology used for these varied widely. Performance indicators, performance evaluation, evaluation of reference sources using check-list, Evaluation of Information Retrieval systems using Precision and Recall rations, Cost-Benefit and cost effectiveness studies, user surveys electing opinions on library services-all these studies make part and parcel of Quality Studies using different mechanisms of assessment and methodologies. In early 1980s, numerous studies were made on automated data validation, error rates and patterns, authority control which belongs to quality control in online databases.

However, customer and employee satisfaction are main focus. Quality assurance studies were mostly restricted to special libraries and academic libraries. Although quality assurance studies based on ISO 9000 and other accreditation schemes were conducted in libraries in UK, USA and Canada, such studies are rarely reported in Indian libraries and information systems. The quality assurance initiative in LIS has primarily come from the parent organization to which it provides services. However, in the later years, the quality assurance system has become as essential feature of LIS management. Quality studies in LIS sector are mostly isolated and are made on different aspects of library management, services, user-studies, etc. The evidence produced by the few TQM cases in the LIS sector indicates that TQM is a highly relevant management theory for information sector.

A library should focus on providing the best services possible, and be willing to change to serve its customers. To determine if changes need to be made, a library administrator might ask: What are our niche markets? What do the customers come in for? How can I look at the efficiency of my library? How do we serve the current customers that exist today? First learn about the customer, and then solve the problems.

ROLE OF LIBRARY MANAGERS IN TQM

Initiating and implementing total quality management programs require great amount of planning and research. Library managers need to get trained in various TQM practices before implementing the same. There are costs involved with the entire process of total quality management. It is the library manager's responsibility to allocate budgets for TQM at the beginning of every financial year. Remember, you can't crib later on. Read a lot about total Quality management. You need to be convinced first why quality is such an important parameter in every business. If you yourself are not convinced, it would be very difficult for you to convince other departments for implementing TQM. Know who your customers are? Understand your target market carefully. Go out, meet customers and find out as to what all they expect from your brand. Customer feedbacks play an important role in formulating strategies for total quality management. As a library manager; you need to work closely with the senior management, human resource professionals to develop foolproof implementation strategies. Remember, a manager has to act as a bridge between the senior management and the entire workforce.

The role of a library manager is to act as a facilitator at the workplace. It is your duty to assist employees in implementing TQM. As a library manager, it is your responsibility to select and appoint right individuals who can work as line managers and take charge of the entire project. The employees, you select ought to be reliable and diligent and should be capable enough to handle a crucial project like total quality management. It is the library manager's responsibility to assign resources for total quality management, allocate time for various training programs and appreciate employees who come up with various improvement ideas and strategies which would help the organization deliver superior quality products. Further train your subordinates to ensure smooth implementation of TQM without any obstacles.

A library manager must communicate the benefits of total quality management to all other members of the organization. Call employees on a common platform and address the benefits and importance of total quality management. Make them understand how successful implementation of total quality management programs would yield high quality products which would not only benefit the organization but also the employees associated with the same. Why do we always think of outsourcing trainers? Why can't we train employees on our own? Believe me, as a library manager if you train your employees, the results would be better rather than an unknown face coming and loading them with information. Do not forget, a trainer needs to be prepared for every question. Do your homework carefully.

Remember, a library manager is always a strong source of inspiration for other employees. You need to practice total quality management yourself before expecting others to believe in the same. Customer feedbacks should be carefully monitored and taken into consideration while formulating company's major strategies. Provide frequent reports to staff members highlighting scope of improvement.

PRINCIPLES OF TQM IN LIBRARIES

The purpose of this paper is to present an overview of total quality management (TQM) in the academic library and information sectors. Education and training are fundamental for the successful implementation of TQM (Deming, 1988). TQM requires employee's participation, each employee needs to learn and understand the underlying principles of TQM. Employees need to have the right skills and they should be granted a platform that enables them to implement the principles of TQM. The objectives of this study are framed based on the extensive literature-search on customer expectations, perceptions, and service quality. The main objectives of the study are to measure customer expectations and quality of the service perceived by the customers. The specific objectives of this study are to: Deming's 14 Points on Quality Management, a core concept on implementing total quality management, is a set of management practices to help organizations increase their quality and productivity. These 14 points are the keys to measure monitor and improve the performance of all organizations. These are slightly meeting the need of the libraries:

- Create constancy of purpose for improving products and services.
- Adopt the new philosophy.
- Cease dependence on mass inspection to achieve quality.
- End the practice of awarding business on price tag alone; instead, minimize total cost by working with a single supplier.

- Improve constantly and forever every process for planning, production and services.
- Institute modern methods of training on the job.
- Institute modern methods of supervision and leadership.
- Drive out fear.
- Break down barriers between staff areas of the departments.
- Eliminate numerical goals for the work force.
- Eliminate work standards and numerical quotas.
- Remove barriers to pride of workmanship, and eliminate the annual rating or merit system.
- Institute a vigorous program of education and self-improvement for everyone.
- Put everybody in the company to work accomplishing the transformation. The transformation's is everybody job.

ELEMENTS OF TQM

Some of the important elements of total quality management are: (i) Management's commitment to quality (ii) Customer satisfaction (iii) Preventing rather than detecting defects (iv) Measurement of Quality (v) Continuous improvement (vi) Corrective action for root cause (vii) Training (viii) Recognition of high quality (ix) Involvement of Employees and (x) Benchmarking.

1. Management's commitment to quality : If an organisation is serious about implementing TQM, the lead has to be taken by the top management with full commitment. It must initiate quality improvement programmes. The top management should continue all the efforts and provide the resources to continue quality improvement programmes. This is provided by collecting, reporting and use of quality related cost information.

2. Customer satisfaction : TQM is designed in such

a manner so as to meet the expectations of customers. In the present era, customer is the king. It must be recognised that customers are the most important persons for any business. The very existence of an organisation depends on them. They are the life blood of a business and deserve the most courteous and affectionate treatment.

3. Preventing rather than detecting defects : TQM checks the poor quality products or services rather than simply to detect and sort out defects. "Prevention rather than detection" is the main characteristic of TQM. Some of the important techniques of TQM which aim at the prevention of defects rather than the detection of the defects are statistical process control, continuous process improvement and problem solving and system failure analysis etc.

4. Measurement of Quality : Quality is a measurable entity and we must know what current quality levels are i.e. where we are or where we stand in respect of the quality and what quality levels we are aspiring for or where we are going.

5. Continuous improvement : TQM comprises of a continuous process of improvement covering people, equipment, suppliers, materials and procedures. It includes every aspect of an operation in an organisation. In Japan the word "Kaizen" is used to describe the continuous process of improvement. In USA, TQM zero defects and six-sigma are used to describe such efforts.

6. Corrective action for root cause : TQM aims at preventing repetition of problems by identifying the root causes for their occurrence and developing means and corrective actions to solve the problems of the root level. Failure analysis and problem solving skills are very useful techniques in this regard.

7. Training : Proper training programmes have to be undertaken to train the employees for the use of TQM concepts and techniques. Employees have to be provided regular training for continuous improvement.

8. Recognition of high quality : TQM aims at developing long term relationships with a few high quality suppliers rather than those suppliers who supply the inferior goods at the low cost.

9. Involvement of Employees : Involvement of employees means that every employee is completely involved at every step of production process which plays an active role in helping the organisation to meet its targets. Employee involvement and empowerment can be assured by enlarging the employee's job so that responsibility and authority is moved to the lowest level possible in the organisation.

10. Benchmarking : Benchmarking is a systematic method by which organisations can measure themselves against the best industry practices. Benchmarking aims at developing best practices that will lead to better performance. It helps a company to learn and incorporate the best practices into its own operations. Benchmarking is a technique of distinguishing an organization's efforts with the best performance in the field and also to suggest how the gap between the two performances can be removed. Thus, benchmarking is a technique of continuous improvement.

APPLICATIONS OF TQM IN LIBRARIES

This definition is apt and offers Application of total quality management (TQM) in academic library and information services in the new millennium. Libraries adapted management practices simply to give their best in the form of services, products and consultations. Application of TQM is to identify service improvement techniques for an academic library systems and services.

Implementation of TQM in academic library and information services requires change in the mental frame of the employees as well as the executives of the library;

customer segmentation in terms of their needs; service strategy to each user segment within library constraints; and the last but not the least, support from the top management of the academic library is must without this the quality can't be improved. Thus, implementation of TQM requires a changed attitude of employees towards their work. Each employee has to contribute his or her best for achieving the objectives of the department which, in turn, are driven by the objectives of the library.

Everyone has to work hard to meet and exceed the user's requirements for literature and information. The whole philosophy of working environment has to be changed by introducing effective policies and procedures. Successful implementation of TQM requires deciding on the customers to whom an academic library aims to serve, assessing their needs, and deciding on the services, the academic library has to provide to each segment of user's, keeping in terms of finance, staff, documents, and databases. In a TQM effort, all members of an organization participate in improving processes, products, services, and the culture in which they work. The meaning of TQM is customer satisfaction through product or services. The customer in the academic library is user/reader/student. The primary purpose of academic library is to support the teaching, research and other academic programs of its parent organization. An academic library is a part of a service organization which delivers personally to the customers. TQM is at present not emerging as one of the management technique, but also felt very essential by several organizations and disciplines.

Sirkin, suggests some ways a library might use the principles of TQM to enhance library and information services.

- Create service brochures and information kits
- Conduct a user survey about library and information services.

- Improve signage
- Change hours of operation
- Provide a more convenient material return.
- Simplify checkout of material
- Use flexibility in staff assignment
- Co-operate with local government.
- Ask vendors to give products demonstration
- Give new staff a through orientation.
- Create inter departmental library advisory groups.
- Improve the physical layout of the library.
- Track complaints
- Develop an active outreach programme.
- Open satellite offices
- Publicize new or changes services.
- Develop user and staff training materials
- Target services o specific groups.
- Offer electronic document delivery.

BENEFITS OF TQM IN LIBRARIES

TQM leads to a synergy of benefits. Libraries that had TQM processes were better performers that those that did not have TQM processes in place. The study indicated that these libraries have improved employees' relationships and retention, improved operating processes, greater customer satisfaction and increase market. (**Eriksson, 2003**).

This was because libraries empowered all levels of management, including self management at customer level; this was done to manage quality systems, improved quality ultimately resulting in decreased costs and increased productivity. The benefits of TQM are shown below.

1. Benefits for the organizations

- Quality improves defects fall
- Staff is motivated
- Problems resolved faster
- Productivity increases
- Cost reduction

2. Benefit to the customer

- Fewer problems with the product of service
- Better customer care
- Greater satisfaction

3. Benefits to the staff

- Empowerment
- More training, more skills
- More recognition

BEST PRACTICES FOR IMPLEMENTATION OF TQM IN LIBRARIES

Successful implementation of TQM program in libraries can be achieved by adopting a set of TQM best practices. For effective implementation of TQM and better results, following steps are identified:

- Effective leadership
- Customer satisfaction management
- Building quality culture
- Developing high performing processes
- Improving product quality and reliability
- Creativity and innovation
- Building supplier partnerships
- Continuous improvement through measurement of quality
- Eliminating root causes of important failure costs.

BARRIERS OF IMPLEMENTING THE TQM IN LIBRARIES

The implementation of TQM in library organizations provides an opportunity to update and enhance the abilities of the staff to work effectively, yet it is still not free from some barriers. A number of barriers to the implementation of TQM have been encountered in all types of organizations, including libraries. In practice, TQM initiatives are not easy to achieve. TQM fails because of the following reasons:

- Lack of management commitment and management understanding on "Quality".
- Lack of awareness on the benefits of TQM implementation in the organization.
- Inadequate knowledge of TQM and improper understanding of the measurement techniques that are used to measure the effectiveness of TQM implementation.
- Lack of clarity in the guideline, implementation plan and implementation methods.
- Lack of understanding about the positive results of continuous improvement.
- Ignoring the importance of customers.

The libraries are faced with major challenges due to many internal and external changes that are taking place. Libraries are well aware of these changes and they are forced to develop strategic and management philosophies to deal with these challenges. This study reveals that there are considerable barriers and difficulties that libraries were faced with during implementing and sustaining their quality improvement initiative. While TQM clearly has positive aspects, implementing it can have potential challenges as well. **(Jurrow and Barnard, 1993)** identify four barriers to the adoption of TQM in libraries:

- **Vocabulary** : Objections to terms such as 'total',

'quality', and 'management';

- **Commitment :** TQM takes several years to implement and requires a long-term commitment by library managers;
- **Process :** Our culture tends to be impatient and we try to solve problems quickly, to TQM's careful process analysis; and
- **Professionalization :** Professional staff can be resistant to turning over their practices and services to what they perceive as the uninformed whims of the customer.

The following suggestions are made for the implementation of quality in the libraries.

- Quality assurance of academic library and information system should be the part of TQM project.
- There is a need to develop standards/norms for assessing quality of information services with particular reference to the Libraries.
- There is a need to evolve methodologies and mechanisms for improvement of quality information services. This will enhance team building, problem solving, cooperation and innovation.
- More funds to be allocated for studying the quality of information services; and
- Training cf staff members in providing quality information services.

REFERENCES

- Deming, W. E. & Edwards, D. W. (1982). Quality, productivity, and competitive position. Cambridge: Massachusetts Institute of Technology, Center for Advanced Engineering Study.
- Eriksson, H. & Hansson, J. (2003). The impact of TQM on financial performance. Measuring Business Excellence. Vol. 7, No. 1, p. 36-50.

- Hernon, P., & Altman, E. (1996). Service quality in academic libraries. Norwood, N.J.: Ablex Publishing.
- Juran, J. M., Gryna, F. M. & Bingham, R. S. (1974). Quality Control Handbook. New York: McGraw-Hill.
- Jurow, S. & Barnard, S. B. (1993). Introduction: TQM fundamentals and overview of contents. Journal of Library administration, 18(1/2), 1-13.
- Sirkin, A.F. (1993). Customer service: another side of TQM. Journal of Library Administration. 18(1/2), 71-83.
- Tann, J. (1993). Dimensions of quality in library setting, Proceedings of a seminar held in Stamford, 1993, edited by M. Ashcroft and d. Barton. Stamford: CPI.
- Van House, N., Weil, B.T. & McClure, C.R. (1990). Measuring academic library performance: a practical approach. Chicago, IL: ALA. 1990.
- Weinberg, G. M. (1991). Quality software management: Volume 1. Systems thinking1. New York: Dorset House.

QUALITY STANDARDS

INTRODUCTION

The library users in today's context expect an effective and efficient service. Providing information for them to satisfy their requirements has become a challenge for librarians and information professionals. With the new developments in information technology, the library functions are being subjected to a wide transformation from its conventional role to suit new environments. Therefore it is important to pay attention to manage the libraries and information centers effectively to provide the maximum services to its users with the available resources. Quality management has been applied within the manufacturing industry for over two decades.

WHAT IS QUALITY

Quality is defined as "the totality of characteristics of an entity that bear on its ability to satisfy stated and implied needs". A Quality Policy is needed because it speaks of the management's intention, commitment and direction regarding quality. In most cases, it spells out clauses and the procedures that are to be followed to implement quality to fix systems and responsibility for each and every activity.

Quality is important because it assists in a company's effort to meet the expectations of the customer. To maintain quality consistently and for continuous improvement, Quality System standards which are provided in the ISO-9000 series are applicable in business and industry. Within the competitive economic environment, it is necessary to satisfy not only the overt or stated requirements of the customer, but also the implied needs. This is what leads to customer delight, loyalty, and long association which are seen in an improve and growing market share

ISO-9000 ORIGIN

ISO stands for the International Organization for Standardization or International Standards Organization and the ISO-9000 is a series of standards for quality systems devised to help companies establish effective quality assurance systems. The ISO-9000 certification is a mark of conformity that the organization's quality assurance system complies with the specific and relevant ISO-9000 standards.

This series was introduced in 1987 by the ISO in Geneva and revised in 1994. This series consists of a set of documents, some providing standard guidelines, and some the actual standards which can be used to develop the quality system. There are five standards in the ISO-9000 series ISO-9000 to ISO-9004. Appropriate ISO-9000 standards can be selected for implementation, depending upon the nature of operation in an organization. The Indian Standard IS-14000 is the equivalent standard to ISO-9000.

For running a business within India, IS-14000 is enough, but presently, it is not recognized outside India.

ISO-9000 is recognized universally and building a quality management system based on the ISO-9000 series is the single biggest step in ensuring a "strong foundation for future business success".

The ISO-9000 certificate is given by a certifying body, an impartial organization either governmental or non-governmental, possessing the necessary competence and reliability to operate a certification system. The receiving or supplying organization must meet the specified requirements of the relevant ISO-9000. The certificate is like a driving license and, therefore, has a validity period which is presently three years, after which recertification is required.

ASPECTS OF QUALITY SYSTEMS

A good quality system ensures consistency of products and services and guarantees the utilization of i) the same materials, ii) the same equipment. and iii) the same methods or procedures every time in the same way. The Quality System requires that the following norms be observed:

- Define each activity.
- Set the appropriate procedure for the activity.
- Document that procedure.
- Act as per the written procedure.

Thus, a good Quality System makes sure that quality is a part of every activity and quality is everyone's responsibility. In practical terms, the documented procedures ensure that the set activities will be conducted in the same way which leads to consistency of products or services. They also involve in the process all the operators concerned with that activity and thereby assure that the level of quality maintenance is the responsibility of everyone. In library and information centres, one can readily see how this could affect routine activities such as, cataloguing and classification, etc. and translate them into effective and speedy functioning.

STRUCTURE OF ISO-9000

The four standards in the ISO-9000 series a shown below and the appropriate ISO standard can be selected for implementation, depending on the nature of operation of an organization.

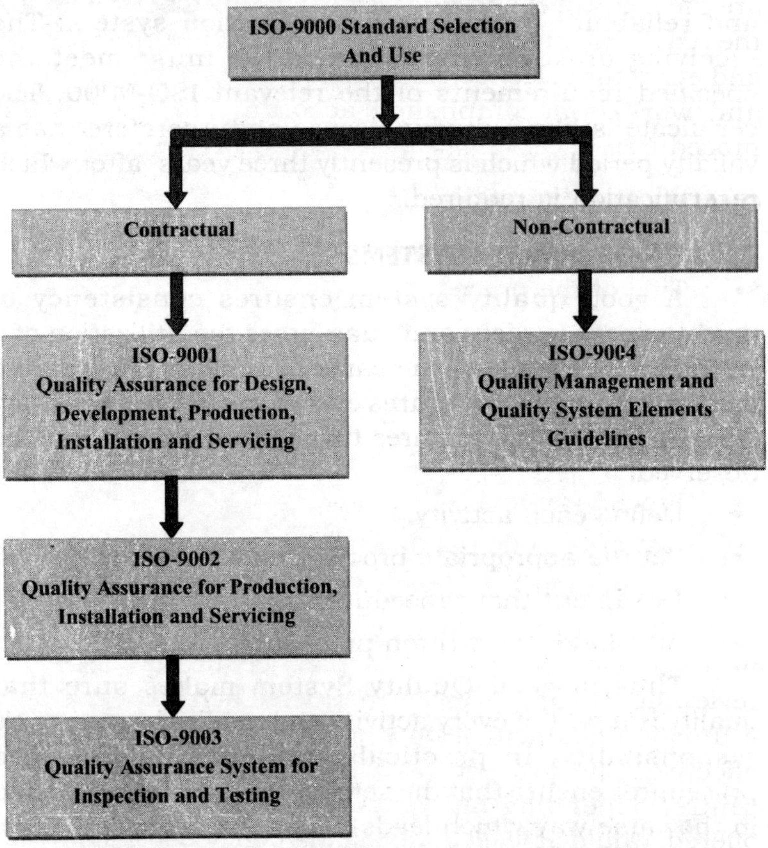

The section of the ISO-9000 series which is most relevant to the library and information services is the element 4.5 of ISO-9001, which is meant for Document and Data control which covers:

- Updating of national and international standards.

- Review and approval of different quality systems documents.
- Availability of the latest issues.
- Removal of obsolete documents.

The philosophy of the Quality Assurance system is that Quality is the hallmark of every operation. Customers are the focus of everything we do. Quality means meeting the requirements of the customer without error first time and every time. Hence, all the activities are written down and work is accomplished according to the written procedures.

QUALITY PROCEDURE

Each procedure has the following facets:

- Title of the procedure.
- Purpose.
- Area of application.
- Definitions, abbreviations and symbols used.
- Responsibility for the procedure.
- Procedure details.
- List of records maintained.
- Circulation list of the controlled copies.

The procedures are prepared by persons involved in a specific activity and each procedure is signed by reviewing and approving authorities. Each procedure has a unique document number and date from which it is effective. The procedures in a library and information centre, depending on the size and variety of services offered, would at least cover acquisition of books, journals and other documents, technical processing or cataloguing/classification of documents, reference or information services, translation services, etc.

ELEMENTS OF ISO-9000

In ISO-9000 which is the most comprehensive in

terms of coverage, there are 20 clauses that need documentation and implementation:

- Management responsibility;
- Quality system.
- Contract review.
- Design control.
- Document and control.
- Purchasing.
- Control of customer supplied products.
- Product Identification and traceability.
- Process control.
- Inspection and testing.
- Control of inspection measuring and test equipment.
- Inspection and test status.
- Control of non-conforming products.
- Corrective and preventive action.
- Handling storage and packaging.
- Control of quality records.
- Internal quality audits.
- Training.
- Servicing.
- Statistical techniques.

Each organization works out methodologies and procedures which must satisfy all these elements.

BENEFITS FROM ISO-9000 CERTIFICATION

Several benefits-tangible and intangible, accrue in obtaining the1SO-9000 certification. The principal of these have to do with confidence in an organization instilled in its current and potential customers. The advantages may be seen as:

- Credibility of the organization goes up.

- Better access to global markets.
- Cost reduction results through eliminating waste, reworking and redundancy.
- Boosting personnel morale by involvement of every employee from top to the bottom.
- Once an organization gets a certificate, its quality system ensures consistency in quality of its output which, in turn, increases customer confidence.
- Internal, external and surveillance audits are part of the quality system and are conducted periodically which help in preventing deterioration and in enhancing quality further.
- Manpower is used more effectively following procedure-task orientation.
- Training new personnel and redeployment of persons to new tasks are also easier.
- Documented procedures are developed by the concerned persons and thus have a higher acceptability.

This leads to improved efficiency, raises employee morale and results in effective communication. However, the benefits of the system must be seen with relation to the high cost of obtaining the certification and it is, thus, more useful for commercial organizations and institutions. The certificate establishes a standard of operation and quality consciousness which is globally recognized.

THE UNIVERSITY LIBRARY QUALITY ASSURANCE SYSTEM

The University Library Quality Assurance System considers eight aspects in evaluation of libraries. They are:

1. Mission and Goals : Mission, goals and objectives serve as the frame work for activities of the University Library Quality Assurance System.

2. Management : Set procedures and mechanisms in normal library activities and responsibility, authority and accountability of staff members in rendering their duties are evaluated here.

3. Resources : Management of physical resources, human resources and library resources is considered.

4. Services : Library services to support University's mission and goals, the services provided for the users, use of new technology in providing the services are considered here.

5. Integration : Integration with other faculties in their academic work and with University management process by taking part in various committees etc. is evaluated.

6. Contribution to academic output : The role of library in academic output in the area of developing information skills of the staff and students of the University.

7. Networking : Corporation with other libraries in providing services and the use of Information Technology in providing remote access etc.

8. Evaluation : Evaluation of library services by user surveys, interviews and requesting for comments and suggestions.

CONCLUSION

The process of acquiring an ISO-9000 certification itself contributes to improving quality in the functioning of an organization. In documenting procedures and operating practices, the organization can streamline various activities and get rid of redundant practices. The preparation of quality and procedure manuals and access to these makes the functioning of the organization more transparent and enhances communication. For corporate library and information centres at least, the adoption of the certification Process makes for more effective working with services and output which are truly relevant to their users.

REFERENCES

- Singh, Uday. N., Jha, K. N & Sinha, Rita (1996). Intellectual property rights in the post industrial society: An Indian perspective. 17th National Seminar of IASLIC, Calcutta.
- ISO-9000 International Standards for Quality Management, Ed 4. ISO, Geneva, 1994.
- Lamprech, James. L. (1992). ISO-9000: Preparing for registration. As & C, *Quality Press*, New York. P. 241.
- Jha, K. N & Sinha, B. N. (1996). Implementation of ISO-9001: Quality system in the information & documentation centre of RDCIS, SAIL. 17th National Seminar of IASLIC, Calcutta.

Unit VI

SYSTEM ANALYSIS AND CONTROL

- ***Systems Analysis** : Introduction, Meaning of System, Definitions of System, Systems Analysis, Analysis, Characteristics of a System, Elements of a System, Types of System, Steps of System Analysis.*
- ***Systems Design** : Introduction, General Considerations, Steps of Design, Conclusion.*
- ***Budgeting** : Introduction, Historical Background of Budget, Meaning of Budget, Definition of Budget, Definition of Budgeting, Essentials of a Budget, Characteristics of Budget, Types of Budgets, Purpose, Functions, Advantages, Principles, Budgeting Techniques of Financial Planning, Budgeting Planning for Library; Budgeting planning factors for Library; Steps for Budgeting Process, Librarian's role under fund crisis, Conclusion.*
- ***Evaluation Techniques** : Introduction, Goals of Evaluation, Types of Evaluation, Evaluation Procedures, Methods of Evaluation, Evaluation Techniques.*

System Analysis And Control

SYSTEM ANALYSIS

INTRODUCTION

Systems are created to solve problems. One can think of the systems approach as an organized way of dealing with a problem. In this dynamic world, the subject System Analysis and Design (SAD) mainly deals with the software development activities.

MEANING OF SYSTEM

The term system is derived from the Greek word 'Systema', which means an organized relationship among functioning units or components.

The dictionary meaning of the word 'System' is, a group of things or parts working together as a whole.

DEFINITIONS OF SYSTEM

A system is a set of entities i.e. men, machines and materials. They form themselves into a system when integrated and bound by a functional relationship to serve a purpose.

A collection of components that work together to realize some objectives forms a system. Basically there are three major components in every system, namely input, processing and output.

System can also be defined as: any combination of relationships combined in a purposeful way.

SYSTEMS ANALYSIS

Systems analysis is then simply the analysis of a system, or it can be defined in any of the following ways:

- A structured technique for handling large, complex problems to lead to an efficient allocation of resources to meet well defined goals and objectives.
- An inquiry to aid the decision maker to choose a course of action by systematically investigating his proper objectives, comparing quantitatively wherever possible the costs effectiveness and risks associated with the alternative policies or strategies for achieving them.
- A viewpoint from which to ask questions.
- A way of thinking

According to Harold Borko, "Systems analysis as a formal procedure for examining a complex process or organization, reducing it to its component parts and relating these parts to each other and to the unit as a whole in accordance with an agreed upon performance criterion'.

According to Verlag Dokumentation, 1976, "Library as a system can be reduced to its component parts and these parts can be related to each other and to the system as a whole according to an agreed upon performance criterion. In the case of the library and information system, increased effectiveness can easily be such a performance criterion. Such an exercise, then, will be a library system analysis".

ANALYSIS

The reduction of the system to its component parts is the beginning of system analysis. Relating these parts to each other and to the Unit as a whole is the completion of the analysis. Such an analysis is undertaken while designing a new system i.e. computerization. Analysis is the starting point for designing a new system. System analysis and design together are thus a single compound concept.

At this stage it is possible to see how the process of system analysis works. Just as a system is reduced to the subsystem comprising it, so also each subsystem is reduced to its component parts. Several interrelated operations carried in a subsystem form its component parts and each of these consists of function, decisions and actions.

CHARACTERISTICS OF A SYSTEM

System suggests some characteristics that are present in all systems: organization (order), interaction, interdependence, integration and a central objective.

1. Organization : Organization implies structure and order. It is the arrangement of components that helps to achieve the objectives. Likewise, a system *i.e.,* a computer system is designed around an input device, .a central processing unit, an output device and one or more storage units. When linked together, they work as a whole system for producing information.

2. Interaction : It refers to the manner in which each component functions with other component of the system.

3. Interdependence : It means that part of the organization depends on one another. One subsystem depends upon the input of another subsystem for proper functioning *e.,* output of one subsystem is the required input for another subsystem.

4. Integration : It is concerned with how a system is tied together. It means that parts of the system work together within the system even though each part performs a unique function.

5. Central Objective : The last characteristic of a system is its central objective. The important point is that user must be known about the central objective of the organization.

ELEMENTS OF A SYSTEM

System has the following elements:

1. Outputs and inputs : A major objective of a system is to produce an output that has value to its user. In order to get a good output, inputs to system must be appropriate. It is important to point out here that determining the output is a first step in specifying the nature, amount and regularity of the input needed to operate a system.

2. Processors : It is the element of a system that involves the actual transformation of input into output. It is the operational component of a system. Processors may modify the input totally or partially, depending on the specifications of the output. In some cases, input is also modified to enable the processor to handle the transformation.

3. Control : The control elements guide the system. It is the decision-making subsystem that controls the pattern of activities governing input, processing, and output.

4. Feedback : Feedback measures output against a standard in some form of cybernetic procedure that includes communication and control. Feedback may be positive or negative, routine or informational. Positive feedback reinforces the performance of the system. It is routine in nature. Negative feedback generally provides the controller with information for action.

5. Environment : The environment is the "supra-system" within which an organization operates. It is the source of external elements that impinge on the system. In fact, it often determines how a system must function.

6. Boundaries and Interfaces : A system should be defined by its boundaries- the limits that identify its components, processes, and interrelationships when it interfaces with another system.

TYPES OF SYSTEM

System has the following types:

1. Physical or Abstract Systems : Physical systems are tangible entities that may be static or dynamic in operation. Abstract systems are conceptual or nonphysical entities. They may be formulas of relationships among sets of variables or models the abstract conceptualization of physical situations.

2. Open or Closed Systems : An open system has many interfaces with its environment. It permits interaction across its boundaries; it receives inputs from and delivers outputs to the outside. A closed system is isolated from environment influences.

3. Man-made Information Systems : An information system is the basis for interaction between the user and the analyst. It provides instructions, commands, and feedback. It determines the nature of relationships among decision makers. From this basis, an information system may be defined as a set of devices, procedures, and operating systems designed around user-based criteria to produce information and communicate it to the user for planning, control and performance

STEPS OF SYSTEM ANALYSIS

The process of system analysis can be considered from two angles. One is from the point of view of problem solving and the other from the point of view of development of new system.

Form the point of view of problem solving the following six basic steps are carried out:

1. Definition and formulation of the problem.

2. Development of alternative solutions.
3. Construction of models which formalize the alternatives.
4 Determine the cost of the design alternatives.
5. Presentation of recommendation.
6. Implementation of the chosen alternatives.

These six steps are schematically represented in figure.

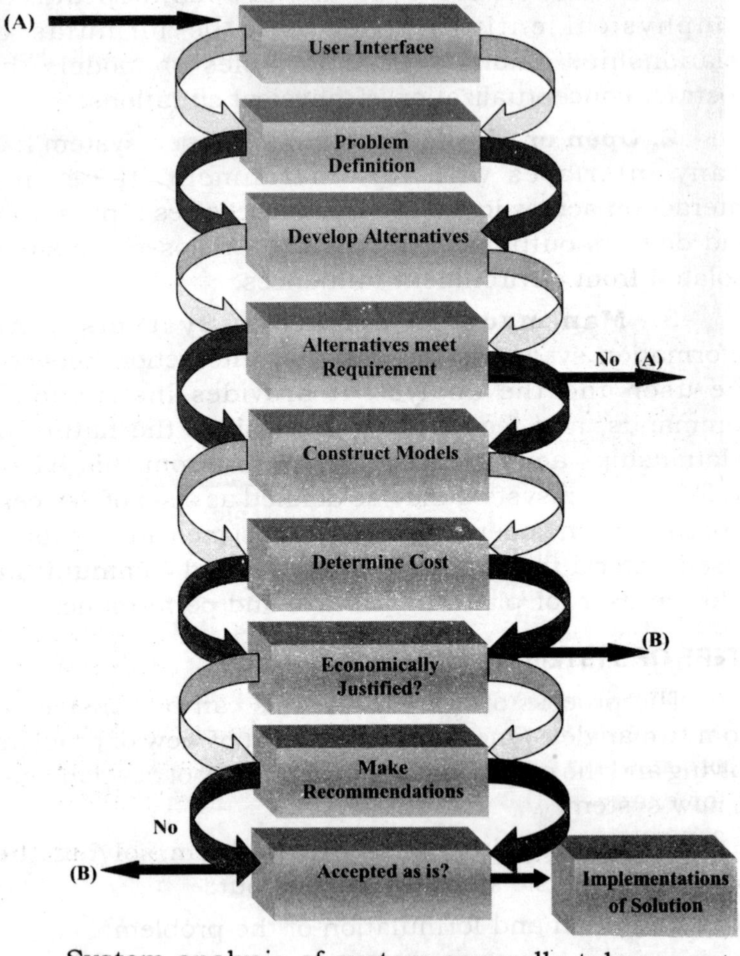

System analysis of system generally takes greater

time period than in the case of problem solving. The activities performed during the development of a system can be identified in three phases:

1. System Analysis
2. System Design
3. System Implementation

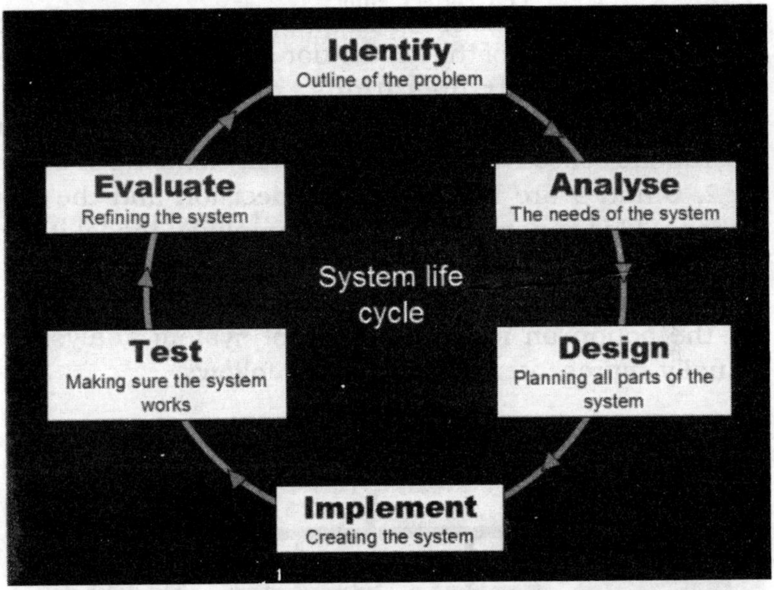

System life Cycle' depicted

Generally, the application of the phases in the life cycle is a highly iterative and interactive ongoing operation, which is usually accomplished at the subsystem level and continues till the total system is modified and eventually supplemented. The functioning of a subsystem on the other hand is a very complex process and it varies from subsystem to subsystem. Take, for example, the acquisitions subsystem and we find it consists of the following operations:

A	**Search**	1. In the library catalogue for availability
		2. In the 'on order' file
		3. If yes, report

	4. If no, proceed
B Accounting	5. Check budget
	6. If no, report
	7. If yes, update expenditure account
C Ordering	8. Version
D Receiving and Checking	9. Check against order
	10. If incorrect, return
	11. If correct, enter

Our analysis of the acquisition sub-system tells that it consists of four operations, namely i.e. search, accounting, ordering, receiving and checking. These four operations collectively consist of eleven elements of which 1, 2, 5 and 9 are functions, 8 is decision and the rest actions. Please note that this is a simplified model it can be more complex. For example, it is possible to insert a step between 3 and 4 where 3 will be a decision followed by the action on it. The process of system analysis is usually represented graphically as follows:

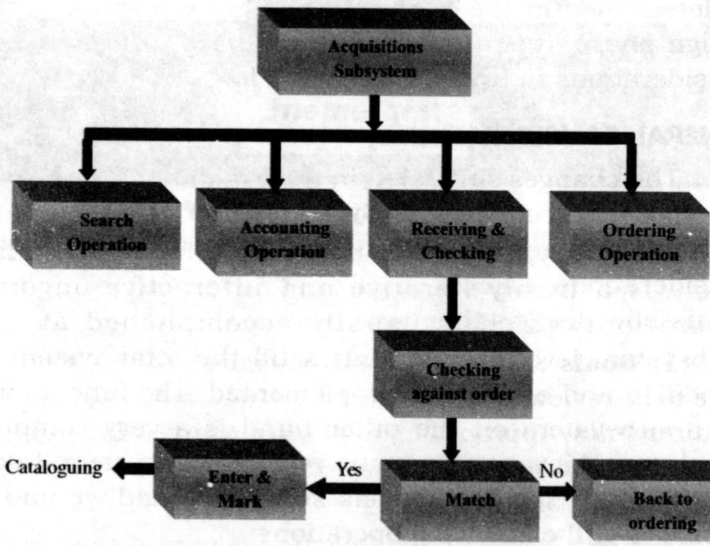

System Analysis of Acquisition Subsystem

The above flow chart does not fail to show the relationship between acquisition and cataloguing subsystem. It also depicts a full analysis of the receiving and checking operation.

SYSTEM DESIGN

INTRODUCTION

Briefly, system design is what a system analysis is undertaken for the analysis phase is the starting point and the design phase is the culmination of the total exercise of systems analysis and design. The existing system is analyzed in order to design an alternative which is thought to be more efficient, more productive and more rewarding. We have seen that an analysis of the existing system results in an evaluation report. The report contains data on the merits and demerits of the existing system as also suggestions on the changes that are necessary for evolving a better system. The design phase, thus, uses the data collected in the analysis phase. What is determined in the analysis phase is validated in the design phase. It is advisable to first discuss the general considerations in systems design.

GENERAL CONSIDERATIONS

The changes suggested in the evaluation report are in fact the corrective measures that ought to be adopted. These measures are adopted in the light of three considerations, namely goals, cost factor and unit cost. Let us now discuss them one by one.

1. Goals : The goals and objectives of the system have to be reviewed with reference to new and augmented requirements. Appropriate modifications in either or both are made in order that the projected system may achieve the desired goals.

2. Cost Factor : Establishing a new system may mean a large capital outlay and increased incurring expenditure. For example, the computer and the peripherals, stationery and the personnel demand non recurrent as well as recurrent financial support. The cost factor is, thus very significant. The economic feasibility of the projected system has to be studied. Such a study will enable the management to take the decision about establishing the alternative system, either as desired or as possible.

3. Unit Cost : The estimated unit cost of each output from the projected new system is compared with the existing unit cost. If the new system can cut considerably, its establishment is amply justified. For example, the cost of cataloguing a book in American libraries came down to $ 1.5 from $ 15 after the establishment of OCLC network. This is the parameter of unit cost that is of great importance in design making.

STEPS OF DESIGN

If the analysis phase results in the determination of requirements, the design phase is concerned with the validation of these requirements to meet the system's revised goal, with the revision of goals there is revision of outputs and consequently of inputs. Thus, the difference between the analysis and the design is of approach only. In the design phase, new procedures are worked out to meet the projected requirement. The elements of the system remain unchanged. The subsystem and the operations are these elements. Basically the design phase consists of the following four steps.

The First Step : In this, all functions are preplanned so that they may be correlated. The preplanning helps to eliminate duplication of records and ensure a logical sequence of all activities to be performed. Because of the interdependence among workers the authority of the heads of subsystem is defined in order to increase the operational effectiveness of the heads of system. New worksheets in place of old ones are prepared. The new work sheets state new requirements and modified outputs to meet them.

The Second Step : As the second step of designing all procedures conceived are reduced to writing. They are described in detail in a logical sequence and supported by flow charts. This is done for each operation. The description and flow charts together comprise the procedural manual. The manual covers all activities and illustrates the flow of work.

The Third Step : This step is devoted to designing appropriate manual procedures. Manual procedures exist and are indispensable even in a highly computerized library system. Information has to be gathered and transformed as input. Even outputs have to be processed manually. Good manual procedures, when described fully, are very helpful in transforming the system from manual to automate. At this stage it is also necessary to ensure the appropriateness of procedures. For example, they should furnish the outputs needed, have a definite purpose in the generation of outputs, justify each function, establish a smooth work flow, and prevent bottlenecks. The procedures should also ensure the full use of available equipment.

The Fourth Step : This step consists in designing the printed forms. These are used in transmitting information and storing and avoiding its repetitive transcription. The design of forms is, therefore, guided by requirements and decisions. The forms should be so designed as to allow the recording of information item by item in the logical order of elements. A single form as far as possible should serve several purposes i.e. book order form can be at the same time used as:

1. On-order record
2. Process slip
3. Notification to the requestor

The form should provide for checking of boxes and should keep writing to the minimum and should be of standard size to facilitate filling. Wherever economical, commercially available forms can be adopted, if they meet the data needs of the system. Lastly, the form should be redesigned if necessary.

If the forms are prepared observing the above principles, they will serve the purpose well. The most important principle here is that the same data required at various points in the system should be recorded at one time only.

A new system is thus designed on the basis of the evaluation report brought out at the end of the analysis phase. What is determined in the analysis is validated in the design.

If necessary, either the goals or functions or both are revised in the light of the objectives and requirements. Procedures are then drawn setting all operations and all steps in each operation in the logical order. The cost factor is taken into account economic feasibility is studied and the design is completed step by step.

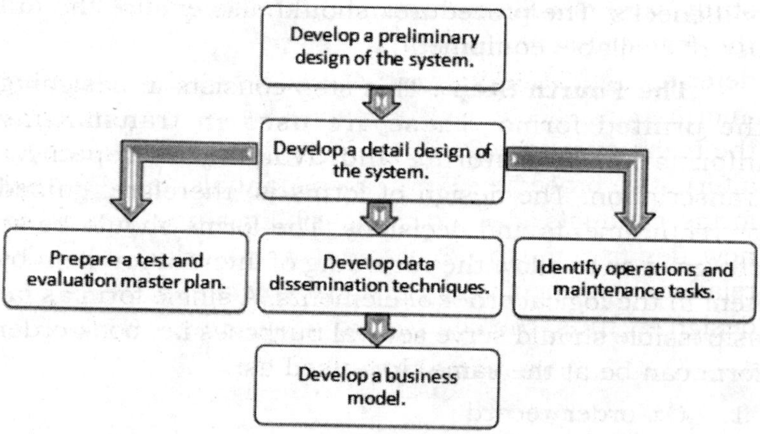

CONCLUSION

System analysis consists in reducing a system to its component parts and relating them to each other and to the system. This is done with reference to an agreed upon performance criterion. It, therefore, follows that, with the recognition of the needs for improvement a system analysis becomes necessary. A system analysis, thus, starts with the objectives and goals and determines the requirements of the system, examines the functions, decisions and actions performed in it, identifies the bottlenecks and suggests alternatives that should yield better results. The analysis so completed comes out with an evaluation report.

The evaluation report contains data on the strengths and weaknesses in the existing system as also the suggestions on the possible changes that are necessary for evolving a better system. Systems analysis obviously means systems approach in evaluation. Since every operation in a system is related to and dependent upon, other operations, no evaluation of an operation in isolation of other operations is worthwhile. Since library is a system, it is amenable to system analysis.

If system analysis is the starting point of system study, systems design is the culmination of it. It gives the framework for a new system. It validated what is determined in the analysis. It uses the same data and information collected in the analysis of the system. It uses the techniques of work sheets and flow charting to build alternative procedures, prepares manuals, develops new forms, conducts an economic feasibility study, determines new department to department and worker to worker relationships and if necessary, even restates goals. System design is, thus, the completion of systems study.

BUDGETING

INTRODUCTION

A single item of public expenditure or that of public revenue cannot be judged in isolation. Whereas public expenditure is designed to promote welfare, the taxes impose costs on the tax payers. The welfare and costs, utility and disutility of government financial transactions, need to be balanced. The demands for expenditure have to be balanced against the available resources. A budget is therefore, a financial plan for rationing scarce resources amongst various demands for expenditure. Over the last few decades, however, budgets have become extremely complex and pervasive. According to Gladstone "they are no longer affairs of arithmetic but in a thousand ways go to the root of prosperity of individuals, the relations of classes and strength of kingdoms. Thus the concerns of budget makers are not just financial, that is, producing a balance between expenditure and revenues; rather these are economic, political, social and administrative in nature.

HISTORICAL BACKGROUND OF BUDGET

Budget word was first coined by the British Kings in early days from the word 'BOUGETTE' which means leather bag or pouch that held the seal of the medieval court exchequer and from which chancellor of exchequer took out papers pertaining to government's financial scheme for ensuring year in front of the parliament.

MEANING OF BUDGET

A budget is a statement containing a forecast of revenues and expenditures for a period of time, usually a year. It is a comprehensive plan of action designed to achieve the policy objectives set by the government for the coming year. A budget is a plan and a budget document is a reflection of what the government expects to do in future. While any plan need not be a budget, a budget has to be necessarily a plan. It shows detailed & location of resources and other measures for their realization.

DEFINITION OF BUDGET

According to Finkler, 1984 a budget is defined as "A budget is a tool for planning, quantifying the plans and controlling costs".

According to Carruth, 2000 "A budget is a plan that uses numerical data to predict the activities of an organization over a period of time and it provides a mechanism for planning each unit's needs and contributions".

A budget is a comprehensive plan in writing, stated in monetary terms that outline the expected financial consequences of management's plans and strategies for accomplishing the organization's mission for the coming period.

DEFINITION OF BUDGETING

Wildavsky, 1986, "Budgeting is the process of "translating financial resources into human purposes".

Blumentritt, 2006, "Budgeting is a process of identifying, gathering, summarizing and communicating financial information of an organization's future activities".

Budgeting, like any other activity, is subject to the interpretation of each practicing organization. Budgeting is the process of preparation, implementation and operation of budgets decisions into specific projected financial plans for relatively short periods of time.

ESSENTIALS OF A BUDGET

An analysis of the above said definitions reveal the following essentials of a budget:

- It is prepared for a definite future period.
- It is a statement prepared prior to a defined period of time.
- The Budget is monetary and / or quantitative statement of policy.
- The Budget is a predetermined statement and its purpose is to attain a given objective.

A budget, therefore, be taken as a document which is closely related to both the managerial as well as accounting functions of an organization.

CHARACTERISTICS OF BUDGET

As stated earlier, a budget is a blueprint for management action. The following are the common features of budget:

A budget is quantitatively stated : The figures in the budget are expressed in monetary terms. However, the monetary figures are supported by non-monetary information such as units to be sold, units to be purchased and others.

A budget is prepared in advance : A budget must be drawn up before the period to which it refers. Figures produced during or after the period may be important, but they are not part of a budget.

A budget relates to a particular period : Generally, the budget is prepared for one year. However, in the case of a seasonal business, there may be two budgets for each year – a slack season budget and a peak season budget.

A budget is a plan of action : A budget is a plan because it concerns actions to be taken rather than a passive acceptance of future trends. Planning is the establishment of objectives and the formulation, evaluation and selection of the policies, strategies, tactics and action required to achieve the objectives. Like all plans, budgets seldom turn out to be totally correct predictions of the future. Conditions may change during the budget period, which renders the budget to be inaccurate. Even so, budget is useful in guiding the actions of managers.

A budget is an estimation or prediction of profit potential : The budget set forth the expenses and revenues planned during the budget period and thereby reveals its profit potential.

TYPES OF BUDGETS

As budgets serve different purposes, different types

of budgets have been developed. The following are the different classification of budgets developed on the basis of time, functions, and flexibility or capacity.

TYPES OF BUDGETS

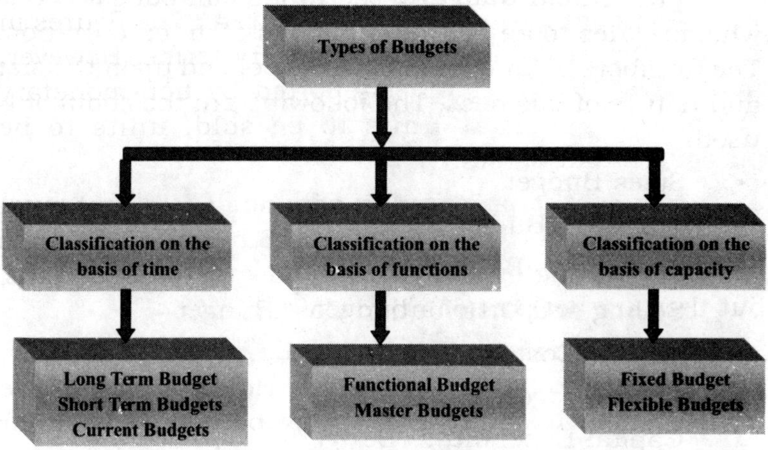

1. Classification on the Basis of Time

Long-Term Budgets : Long-term budgets are prepared for a longer period varies between five to ten years. It is usually developed by the top level management. These budgets summarise the general plan of operations and its expected consequences. Long-Term Budgets are prepared for important activities like composition of its capital expenditure, new product development and research, long-term finance etc.

Short-Term Budgets : These budgets are usually prepared for a period of one year. Sometimes they may be prepared for shorter period as for quarterly or half yearly. The scope of budgeting activity may vary considerably among different organization.

Current Budgets : Current budgets are prepared for the current operations of the business. The planning period of a budget generally in months or weeks. As per ICMA London, "Current budget is a budget which is established for use over a short period of time and related to current conditions."

2. Classification on the Basis of Function

Functional Budget : The functional budget is one which relates to any of the functions of an organization. The numbers of functional budgets depend upon the size and nature of business. The following are the commonly used:

- Sales Budget
- Purchase Budget
- Production Budget
- Selling and Distribution Cost Budget
- Labour Cost Budget
- Cash Budget
- Capital Expenditure Budget

Master Budget : The Master Budget is a summary budget. This budget encompasses all the functional activities into one harmonious unit. The ICMA England defines a Master Budget as the summary budget incorporating its functional budgets, which is finally approved, adopted and employed.

3. Classification on the Basis of Capacity

Fixed Budget : A fixed budget is designed to remain unchanged irrespective of the level of activity actually attained.

Flexible Budget : A flexible budget is a budget which is designed to change in accordance with the various level of activity actually attained. The flexible budget also called as Variable Budget or Sliding Scale Budget, takes both fixed, variable and semi fixed manufacturing costs into account.

PURPOSE OF BUDGETING

- Budget supplies the mechanism for translating fiscal objective into projected monthly spending pattern.
- Budget enhances fiscal planning and decision-making.
- Budget clearly recognizes controllable and uncontrollable cost areas.
- Budget offers a useful format for communicating fiscal objectives.
- Budget allows feedback of utilization of budget.
- Budget helps to identify problem areas and facilitates effective solution.
- Budget provides means for measuring and recording financial success with the objectives of the organizations.

FUNCTIONS OF BUDGETING

An effective budgeting system is vital to the success of a business firm. Budgeting is needed in organizations to perform the following functions:

1. Planning : The budget is a formal planning framework that provides specific deadlines to achieve departmental objectives and contributes towards the overall objectives of an organization. A budget in corporates expected performance and present managerial targets. Budgeting influences the formulation of all business strategies and subsequently assists business managers in executing such strategies.

2. Coordination : Coordination is a managerial function under which all factors of production and all departmental activities are balanced and integrated to achieve the objectives of the organization. Budget helps management to coordinate in the following ways:

- The existence of a well laid plan is the major step towards achieving coordination. Executives' are forced to think of the relationships among individual operations, and the company as a whole.

- Budgets help to restrain the empire-building efforts of executives. Budgets broaden individual thinking by helping to remove unconscious biases on the part of engineers, sales and production officers.
- Budgets help to search out weaknesses in the organizational structure. The Formulation and administration of budgets isolate problems of communication, of fixed responsibility, and of working relationships.

3. Communication : It is necessary in an efficient organization that all people be informed about the objectives, policies, programmes and performances. Budgets inform each manager of what others have agreed to do. They also inform managers of the resources available to achieve objectives and targets.

4. Control and performance evaluation : Budgeting enters into control at three following points:

- When a budget is being formulated, departments analyse their plans for the future and submit estimates as per their requirements, justifying each of their demands by demonstrating a need.
- After budgets of different departments have been reviewed and approved they become targets that desirable limits on spending.
- At the end of the budget period, a comparison of actual expenditures with budget expenditure is made as a means of judging performance and fixing responsibility for deviations. Budgets are the basis of performance evaluation in an organization as they reflect realistic estimates of acceptable and expected performance.

ADVANTAGES OF BUDGETING

- Budgeting compels and motivates management to

make an early and timely study of its problems. It generates a sense of caution and care, and adequate study among mangers before decisions are made by them.

- Budgeting provides a valuable means of controlling income and expenditure of a business as it is a "plan for spending".
- Budgeting provides a tool through which managerial policies and goals are periodically evaluated, tested and established as guidelines for the entire organization.
- Budgeting helps in directing capital and other resources into the most profitable channels.
- Budgeting coordinates and correlates all business activities. It enables management to decentralize responsibility without losing control of the business.
- It provides a norm, basis or yardstick for measuring performance of departments and individuals working in organizations.
- Budgeting encourages productive competition, provides incentive to perform efficiently and gives a sense of purpose to each individual in the organization.
- Budgeting, if executed in nearly every enterprise, helps the total national economy by providing stability of employment, economic use of resources and effective prevention of waste

PRINCIPLES OF BUDGETING

1. Be Conservative : Don't budget on the basis that everything will turn out as expected. Build in a safety factor by tending to underestimate one's income and overestimate one's expenses.

2. Consult other people in setting a budget : One person may be responsible for the compilation of the budget but one person should not be responsible for all the work involved. Budgeting requires teamwork. The task of budgeting should be spited and allocated among those individuals who have the best experience of what expenditure is likely to be needed and what income is to be expected. Involvement of many people in budgeting might slow down the process, but the answer is far more likely to be accurate and dependable.

3. Allow plenty of time : Budgeting is not an activity that can be completed in a few hours. A good budget may be worked on for several weeks if not months, adding and changing figures as new information comes to light.

4. Budget estimates should be cash based : It means that estimation of expenditure and income should related to what is expected to be actually spent or received during the year and not to liability or demands which have incurred or would incur within the year but to be realized in some other years.

5. Budget revenue and capital portions should be kept distinct : The third principle of budgeting making is that distinction between recurring expenditure and income on the one hand and capital payment on the other hand should be maintained and the two shown in two separate parts of budget.

6. Estimation should be as closed as possible : It means that estimation should be as exact as possible. Over estimation would lead to heavy taxation and under estimation is achieved by taking past three years average figures one aids to close budgeting.

7. The form of estimates should correspond to the form of accounts : It means that budgetary heads should be as same as those of accounts. This facilitates budget preparation, budgetary and account keeping.

8. Rule of lapse : The rule says that any part of the grant not spent within the financial year cannot be kept for future and should be returned.

9. Excellence in documentation : It is very important that the author of the budget strives to produce documents that can be read and understood by anyone. If figures are not clearly labeled even the author will, as time passes have trouble understanding where the figures came from and how the calculations were made. It should be assumed that budgeting will be:

- Circulated too many different people who may have lower levels of financial literacy.
- Useful again in a year's time when the budgeting process begins again. Unless documents are well labeled it may be difficult to remember.

BUDGETING TECHNIQUES OF FINANCIAL PLANNING

Budgeting refers to a course of action based upon an estimate of assumed income and expenses. It is simply a term is defined as a plan of operation where one reviews their income and expenditures, often in the effort to create a strategy in order to achieve some financial goal or goals within a specific period of time. There are numerous budgeting techniques found in practice. Some of them are often used in the library. These are:

1. Line by line budgeting
2. Formula budgeting
3. Program budgeting
4. Performance budgeting
5. Planning Programming Budgeting System
6. Zero Based Budgeting

1. Line by line budgeting

Line-item budgeting is probably the most common budgeting system. It makes all increases and decreases to the budget equal for all units on a percentile basis. Basically, there is a line for every type of expenditure e.g. library materials, electricity, travel, and a numbering system to keep track of them. The great problem with line-item budgeting is that they don't show the true costs of services or programs, which are comprised of several line items. And the individual line items each support several programs. Line item budgeting is very easy to cut with no real accountability for the consequences.

Advantages of a Line-Item Budgeting

- **Easy to Make :** From a technical standpoint, it's easy to create a line-item budget. With a piece of lined paper and a pencil, you can list all expenses, giving each item its own line and specific dollar amount. This is why many organizations, especially very small businesses, choose line-item budgeting. It is straightforward and does not require linking budgeting to advanced accounting, such as activity-based costing, or management practices, such as performance-based budgeting.
- **Micro-Level Expense Control :** Line-item budgets offer advantages for managers seeking to control expenses at the operational level. For example, the executive in a human resources department might want to trim expenses on applicant drug testing. So he can give employees in HR a reduced line item for testing for the next year to reinforce a new policy that only an applicant who has accepted a job offer and agreed to a start date can take a drug test at the employer's expense.
- **Flexible Control :** Line-item budgeting can give a large organization flexible use of budgetary control, giving flexibility to some programs and not others based on defined criteria. For example, if line items are broad in scope, such as facility operations, salaries and benefits, and administrative costs, an administrator could write her own line items under each broad item. A school principal could use a broad line item for salaries to choose the number of teachers, professional staff and support staff to hire each school year according to the school's needs as long as this staffing plan fits the total salary funding level and applicable laws.

- **Reliance of Past Data:** Line-item budgeting is easy to model after past budgets and other historical data. When writing a line-item budget, the budget maker can consider whether program sites, business activities and departments should receive the same level of funding as the previous year or an increase or decrease by line item. Historical data might include sample budgets from other organizations. For example, the principal of a new elementary school could begin with the budget of another elementary school in the same district with the same enrollment and curriculum offerings.

2. Formula based budgeting

Formula budgeting is typically used by the government bodies as a means of distributing its money to its sub units. A formula is essentially asset of predefined rules accepted by the authority. When formula budgeting is used in a particular institution, different formulas are used for different units. For example, the library and physics lab would probably have different formulas for budgeting as part of the college. Some of the factors that are consider for formula budgeting are number students users, space coverage, number of services provided etc.

3. Program based budgeting

A budget prepared with program descriptions instead of expense line items. Programme budgeting, developed by U.S. president Lyndon Johnson, is the budgeting system that, contrary to conventional budgeting, describes and gives the detailed costs of every activity or programme that is to be carried out with a given budget. In Britain it is referred to as 'Output Budgeting'. It is mainly useful to government departments and non-profit organizations. In programme budgeting special emphasis is laid on formulation of different budgets for different programmes. It utilizes a planning and budgeting process in an output oriented programme format which is oriented to its objectives to facilitate developing and evaluating alternatives. It leads to the allocation of resources over a planning period. Programme budgeting integrates all the organization's planning activities and budgeting into a total system.

Programme budgeting is the short form for Planning, Programming and Budgeting System (PPBS). This is a budgetary process meant for making operation more effective and efficient, through improved allocation of resources. It aims at optimum utilization of available scarce resources so that maximum benefit can be derived. Budgets are prepared for the different programmes of the library such as administrative services, technical services, readers' services, reference services etc. Cost-benefit analysis is carried out for each programme so that most favorable can be selected out of alternative sub-programmes. PPBS is mainly used in non-profit organizations to enable them to make more improved decisions about resources allocation. For example, if an academic library system is planning a 'Request an Article' service for their users, then the cost of the service in term of staffing, materials documents is calculated and presented.

4. Performance based budgeting

Performance budget aims to evaluate performance of various responsibility units. This method measures the quantity of performed activities. For example, data on the number of books acquired, classified and catalogued, actual man hours work for circulation service etc. The quality of performance of the activities is very difficult to measure in terms of money costs. Careful accumulation of data over a certain period of time is essential to this approach. It requires cost-benefit analysis to established priorities. Costs are presented in term of work to be accomplished, so that the emphasis is on cost at the expense of service. The great difficulty of performance budgeting is to classify all operations into functions, programmes and activities.

Process of Performance Budgeting

Performance budgeting is a technique or a method employed by any agency/department. The first stage is to decide what its goal or objective should be, the next stage is to decide on a set of programmes in order to achieve the goal and then to implement the programme. Final stage is to evaluate the actual performance of each segment and its contribution towards achievement of its goal.

Operational Steps in Performance Budgeting

- Formulation of objectives of the agency/department.
- Identification of various programmes or projects, which will help the agency to achieve its objective.
- Evaluation of the programmes in terms of benefits that they produce compared to the resources that they consume.
- Selection of the programmes on the basis of cost benefit analysis in order to utilize the funds in the optimal manner.
- Development of performance criteria for the various programmes (suitable work measurement units, norms, yardsticks, standards, and other performance indicators).
- Preparation of long-term physical as well as financial plans.
- Preparation of the annual budget.
- Assessment of performance of each programme and by each responsibility unit and comparison of the same with the budget.

5. Planning Programming Budgeting System

Planning, Programming, and Budgeting System (PPBS) is in effect an integration of a number of techniques in a planning and *budgeting* process for identifying, costing and assigning a complexity of resources for establishing priorities and strategies in a major program and for forecasting costs, expenditure and achievements within the immediate financial year or over a longer period.

6. Zero Based Budgeting

Zero-based budgeting (ZBB) is a method of budgeting in which all expenses must be justified for each new period. A zero-based budgeting start from a zero bases and every function within an organization is analyzed for its needs and costs. ZBB affords a choice amongst the alternatives so that activities would be selected in order of their importance. It facilitates identification of inefficient and unnecessary activities to avoid wasteful expenditure of the library. Librarians must first identify the priorities and justify their costs. ZBB works as follows:

- The work in the library is broken up into units i.e. circulation, journals, books, etc.
- Priorities of units are established based on goals and objectives of the organization.
- Cost of operating each unit is worked out.
- Each unit then ranked in priority order and presented for approval or rejection.
- Finally approved or rejected based on affordability.

Zero Based Budgeting Steps

1. Identification of a task.
2. Finding ways and means of accomplishing the task.
3. Evaluating these solutions and also evaluating alternatives of sources of funds.
4. Setting the budgeted numbers and priorities.

Zero Based Budgeting Advantages

1. Accuracy : Against the regular methods of budgeting that involve just making some arbitrary changes to the previous year's budget, zero-based budgeting makes every department relook each and every item of the cash flow and compute their operation costs. This to some extent helps in cost reduction as it gives a clear picture of costs against the desired performance.

2. Efficiency : This helps in efficient allocation of resources (department-wise) as it does not look at the historical numbers but looks at the actual numbers.

3. Reduction in redundant activities : It leads to the identification of opportunities and more cost-effective ways of doing things by removing all the unproductive or redundant activities.

4. Budget inflation : Since every line item is to be justified, zero-based budget overcomes the weakness of incremental budgeting [hyperlink to be put] of budget inflation.

5. Coordination and Communication : It also improves co-ordination and communication within the department and motivates employees by involving them in decision-making.

Zero Based Budgeting Disadvantages

1. Time-Consuming : Zero-based budgeting is a very time-intensive exercise for a company or a government funded entries to do every year as against incremental budgeting, which is a far easier method.

2. High Manpower Requirement : Making an entire budget from the scratch may require the involvement of a large number of employees. Many departments may not have an adequate time and human resource for the same.

3. Lack of Expertise : Explaining every line item and every cost is a difficult task and requires training the managers.

BUDGETING PLANNING FOR LIBRARY

Budgeting means the act of drawing or preparing budget in a concern for a fixed future period. It is the task or functions of drawing up statements in planning for estimated revenues and corresponding expenses of a concern for a fixed future period. It is not a day or two or by mere oral discussion, but is a continuous job. The library has endeavored to maintain a balance, effecting budget for collections and services as well as to positions, and to make choices that offer the prospect of rebuilding recognized areas of strength once the financial conditions improve. Before going to prepare the library budget, a librarian must:

- Understand the values, strategy and plans of the library.
- Understand what it means to be cost effective and cost efficient.
- Understand what is involved in generation and rising funds.

BUDGETING PLANNING FACTORS FOR LIBRARY

The preparation of budget and implementation of budgetary control in a modern library requires an effective budget programme with the help of a sound and efficient organization. The following are the principal budget planning factors generally considered for the better functioning of budget organization.

1. Budget period : A budget period is a period of time for which the budget is prepared and operated. There is no hard and fast rule for the selection of budget period. The budget period may be (i) short term- a period of one year or less, (ii) medium term- two or three year period, and (iii) long term- more than five year period. Generally long term budget is prepared for construction of library building. Medium term budget is generally preparing for purchase of stacks, furniture etc. and short term budget for acquisition of books, journal, annual maintenance charges etc.

2. Budget committee : Budget committee is a committee formed with few members for formulation of a general programme for preparing budget and for exercising overall control over implementation of the budget. A budget committee will provide guidelines for preparation of functional budgets evaluate and revise the estimates before preparing the final budget and prepare master budget.

3. Budget manual : A budget manual is a written document, book-let or schedules indicating the policy of the budget, objectives of budget organization, procedures to be followed in budgeting, forms to be used and the responsibilities to be created at different levels. A budget manual provides the rules and instructions for budgeting, routine and procedures and all other affairs regarding budgetary control. So a budget manual indicates what to do, how to do, when to do and in which form to do.

4. Budget centre : The budget centre is a section of the organization for the responsibility of executing the budget will be fixed. Library is to be treated as a cost centre of the college. The main objective of setting up budget centre is to judge whether costs are controlled at the point of occurrence or not.

5. Organization chart : An organization chart is chart used in budgeting and budgetary control showing the authority and responsibilities of each members of the budget committee with the other members in the committee. So an organization chart shows the scope of authority and responsibility of the members and their inter-relationship at a glance.

6. Limiting factor : Limiting factor or key factor in budgeting is that factor which influences directly to the preparation of a functional budget and extent of whose influence must be assessed first of all. There may have only one or more limiting factor for the library budget. The limiting factors are to be identified and diagnosed carefully at the time of budgeting because the budget will be meaningless or purposeless unless these are not considered in depth. The fund, space, library staff etc. are the some limiting factors which should be consider at the time of preparation of library budget.

STEPS FOR BUDGETING PROCESS

These common steps can be listed as follows:

1. Obtaining Estimates : Obtaining estimates of sales, production levels, expected costs, and availability of resources from each sub-unit/division/department: The departmental heads or managers are required to provide estimates of future conditions and activities that will have an impact on the company. The discussion and participation may be in the form of informal discussions and/or detailed written reports of plans which will be submitted to the budget committee for approval.

2. Coordinating estimates : In many organizations, the budget committee evaluates the different plans submitted by various organizational units to determine the potentiality of plans in the overall interest of the company and to estimate what resources are available and can be fairly allocated among the various units of the organization.

3. Communicating Budget : Communicating the budget to responsible managers and the concerned departments: After individual budget plans have been approved in the light of organizational goals and availability of resources, the budgets should be communicated to departments and responsible managers. Changes and modifications incorporated in the final budget should be made known to managers to obtain their cooperation and support for the budgets. Budgeting requires effective communication to convince the departmental manager about changes in the budget.

4. Implementing the Budget Plan : The final budget is presented to the managers concerned and adopted as the plan of operation for the coming budget period. The various service units in a business enterprise are required to provide the necessary materials, labour, facilities and other resources to carry out the budget.

5. Reporting Interim Progress towards Budgeted Objectives : As a feedback in the budgeting process, performance reports are prepared to inform departmental managers and top management about the performances achieved in terms of budgeted figures. Such an investigation may call for a need to revise the budget during the year. For example, it is advisable to reduce production when sales are low than to continue with high production levels. This feedback of information can also be used as a basis for preparing the next year's budget.

LIBRARIAN'S ROLE UNDER FUND CRISIS

The digital revolution boosts the library user's demand for accessing the wide range of library services at 24/7. Again social, economic, educational and technological developments including the growth of social networking, virtual learning and research environments change the traditional library services. Librarians have to face the kinds of financial pressures to outline the above, they have to ensure to providing the high levels of services and continue to same. Librarians have to perform a leading role for the preparation of library budget and implementation which are as follows:

1. Fund acquisition : Librarian should know the sources of fund for library. Internal sources of fund includes college's own grant, photocopying fees, fines for late returns of library documents, sales of old periodicals, movie shows etc. and external sources includes various grants from the external agencies, donations etc.

2. Budget preparation : Librarian should embrace the principle of decentralized budgeting. Departmental heads and subject experts would then be involved in preparing and managing library budgets. This will enhance managerial skills and democratize fiscal management resulting in more transparency and accountability in the library's financial dealings. The budget format should reflect the categories and items that are decided for estimation for the library and must allow for sub-totals and for a total expenditure. Librarian should cultivate the culture of budgeting. Some form of financial management system should be used for the library. No matter how small the resources allotted, a plan must be made and/or implemented.

3. Fund allocation : Proper allocation is essential for better utilization of fund. The collections found deficit would be given high priority in the form of a need based assessment for departmental allocation of fund.

4. Documents acquisition : Librarian should monitor the selection and acquisition of print and electronic resources for the library so that the acquired documents should be highly usable and the fund utilized properly.

5. Allocation control : Budgets are prepared in advance and there is likely to be price increases between the time of preparation and the time when the amount is spent. A handsome consideration should be made at the time of budget estimation. Budget monitoring is required to measure how closely the library is meeting its objectives in terms of its finance. A variance report is to be prepared to compare the actual revenues and expenditure against the budgeted amount for the budgetary control purpose.

6. Long term planning : Long term planning for the library includes extension of library building, acquisition of new furniture and fixtures, purchase of new racks and almirahs etc. Librarian should take active role for the designing of the library layout.

7. Value creation : Fostering an environment in

which students and others can make effective use of library holdings as well as resources held by other institutions.

8. New services : Finally the librarian has to create the facilities to access the electronic subject information with the help of information communication technology. The cost of introducing new library services should be cost effective and long term benefit should be available from there.

CONCLUSION

If the budget has been grooming carefully and steadily with the needs of the library, it will be found that some budgets do not need to be expanded nearly as high. Gather as much information as possible to build budget requests; this is especially important in view of the financial crises we are all facing. Statement supporting budgets must be precise and sensitive to change yet make able to provide continuity.

Again what it means in practiced terms is that librarians will have to become familiar with the concepts and techniques employed in economic planning and some will head to become much more familiar with the educational, social and technological needs of the member served.

Finally management of libraries requires an awareness of the political context in which they operates. It was thought that the fate of libraries and the quality of library services was more affected by extraneous factors such as the authority's attitude, personal grievance, students' militancy etc. than by the library staff.

EVALUATION TECHNIQUES

INTRODUCTION

Evaluation is an attempt to appraise the quality/ suitability of a resource. It is not the same as Assessment. There are many reasons why we might want to perform an evaluation. Here are some of them:

- Selection – which resource is better?
- Monitoring – is our development heading in the right direction?
- Justifying – show something is value for money.
- Validating – did we make the right decision?
- Improving – can we improve if we change something?
- Research – add to a body of knowledge.

GOALS OF EVALUATION

- Assess extent of system functionality
- Assess effect of interface on user
- Identify specific problems

TYPES OF EVALUATION

There are two types of evaluation, viz. formative and summative.

1. Formative Evaluation

This type of evaluation is conducted during the planning and design of the programme. It provides immediate feedback for programme modification and improvement. This type of evaluation is on-going. It helps to determine programme strengths and weaknesses.

2. Summative Evaluation

This is concerned with the evaluation of an already completed programme. When all that has been planned has been done, summative evaluation can be carried out to determine whether the programme has achieved its goals. It is the kind of evaluation that summarizes the strengths and weaknesses of a programme. It may help programme leaders to determine whether the programme is worth continuing. It is done when the programme is considered to be ready for general use. It provides potential consumers with evidence of the value of a programme. It helps to check the effectiveness of the programme.

Formative and summative evaluations are both important, since decisions are needed in the early and final stages of a programme. The early decisions are needed for programme improvement, while the final decisions help to check its worth.

EVALUATION PROCEDURES

The evaluation process involves a series of activities in a sequence. These are:

1. Identification of goals to be assessed : It is important to establish the limits, or variables, for evaluation in the initial stages. This is to say that evaluation can focus on the entire programme or some aspects of it. Such objectives should be clearly stated, concise, specific and measurable. An example of such an objective would be: make students attend a career fair by the end of the first term. This is when the purpose of evaluation is classified, and the issues to be evaluated are identified.

2. Development of an evaluation plan : After the establishment of evaluation objectives, there is a need to identify the most appropriate way of judging the extent to which a programme has achieved its goals and objectives. There should be specific information on how the data is collected, when it is collected, and by whom. This plan must indicate how the data is organized, and to whom it will be sent. It should provide findings on the future development of the programme. At this stage, the evaluation team is identified, and the techniques to be used are selected and designed.

3. Application of the evaluation plan : When the evaluation plan has been approved, it can be put into effect. Its validity or success depends on the competence of the evaluator, its timing, and how effectively it has been planned. There is a need for the plan to be effected by someone who understands what it is intended to do. This is when data collection and analysis take place.

4. Utilization of the findings : Evaluation alone is of little value. It is the application of the findings that makes it worthwhile. Through evaluation, programmes learn their strengths and weaknesses, and the findings offer an opportunity to determine future programme improvements. Adequate use of evaluation findings should be planned, and programme leaders should ensure that they are implemented and followed up. This establishes the extent to which the findings have been incorporated for purposes of programme improvement. A failure to use evaluation findings, adversely affects the programme, and contributes to failure. A follow-up will lead to a review, which will determine whether there is a need for revision of the exercise.

METHODS OF EVALUATION

1. 'Before and After' Method

This is when the programme progress is checked after a given period of time, and it checks the results of specific programme activities. For example, if students are introduced to a computer awareness programme, or career exploration, an evaluation of how much has been covered is carried out by the end of the year. It is at this point that the evaluation may check whether clients are different after the exercise.

2. Comparison Method

This is when groups are compared after different

techniques have been used to achieve a goal. The comparative method may be used to judge the results in groups in different localities, e.g. checking the impact of a programme on rural and urban children, or boys and girls. It may also be used to compare the effects of teacher-pupil ratios on the attainment of goals.

3. The 'How Do we Stand?' Method

This helps to identify desirable programme outcomes. Various techniques are used to check how the programme has progressed in terms of goal attainment. It compares programmes with generally accepted standards, and offers an opportunity to make comparisons. The method compares a programme with a set standard, as there are certain features with which it will be expected to conform.

EVALUATION TECHNIQUES

There are several evaluation techniques or ways of collecting data. It is important for the evaluator to select the best technique to suit the purpose, and choose which programme leaders can be used to check the value of their programmes. These include tests, interviews, observations, and questionnaires, inspection of records, discussions and open box suggestions.

1. Observations : This is a visual technique where the evaluator observes, and records, any findings. Here, the evaluator decides whether he/she will observe as an outsider, or as a participant. This requires full concentration by the observer, who should study an aspect in detail, after consultation with other programme implementers. The observer actually serves as a second person for what other implementers are looking for. For this technique to be worthwhile, the observer should report and discuss any findings immediately, so that possible distortions, or failure to remember, do not affect the results. When using this technique, observers need to have sharp eyes and ears to be able to collect adequate data. The observer should carefully guard against bias.

2. Interviews : Interviews are a basic evaluation technique. They can be structured or unstructured. This requires a good ability to listen. A more structured interview would require the preparation of interview questions prior to the interview itself. It is important that data be recorded. The evaluator may use a tape recorder, in order to transcribe the relevant parts later, or take notes throughout the interview. Some evaluators depend on their memory, but this leads to a great risk of missing out important information. It is important that notes taken are discussed with the person interviewed, to check whether the information was correctly recorded.

3. Questionnaires : This involves a structured series of questions and statements that enable the evaluators to gather information about a particular programme. The advantage is that it can be sent to clients, to be completed in the absence of the evaluator. Unlike an interview, it also gives the evaluator an opportunity to cover a larger number of people at one time. All evaluation techniques require planning on the part of the evaluator. It is important for the evaluator to consult with relevant beneficiaries on the evaluation techniques they would like to use, so that conflicts of interest are avoided.